ROBBIE WILLIAMS

SONG BY SONG

SÉBASTIEN MEROUR

FONTHILL

To Rob JP, my secret Argentinian twin.

Fonthill Media Language Policy

Fonthill Media publishes in the international English language market. One language edition is published worldwide. As there are minor differences in spelling and presentation, especially with regard to American English and British English, a policy is necessary to define which form of English to use. The Fonthill Policy is to use the form of English native to the author. Sébastien Merour was born and educated in France; therefore British English has been adopted in this publication.

Fonthill Media Limited
Fonthill Media LLC
www.fonthill.media
office@fonthillmedia.com

First published in the United Kingdom and the United States of America 2024

British Library Cataloguing in Publication Data:
A catalogue record for this book is available from the British Library

ISBN 978-1-78155-900-0

Typeset in 10pt on13pt Sabon
Printed and bound in England

Contents

Introduction

The public knows Robbie Williams very well: his personality, image, tattoos, and style. But who really knows his songs?

The media often tends to sum up Robbie to a few greatest hits: 'Angels' of course, but also 'Rock DJ', 'Let Me Entertain You', 'Supreme', 'Feel', 'Millennium', 'Come Undone', or 'She's The One' are the most cited tracks, and rightly so: not only are they his greatest hits, but in addition, these songs are almost systematically included by the singer himself into the set lists of his concerts. As a consequence, articles written by journalists about the concerts and the singer constitute an almost impassable wall. Even the fans, for a large majority, will not try to cross this wall, so entertained are they by everything that surrounds the singer: his looks, his voice, his escapades, his provocations, his interviews, his photos, and his humour, especially since the media identify him as the 'King of Entertainment', a title he has obtained since his hit 'Let Me Entertain You', which triumphantly opens each of his gigs.

Yet, what defines a singer? If we put aside for a moment all the artifices or additional skills that a singer can put forward, we must not forget that, originally, a singer sings songs. Yes, the songs are still the basis of a singer's career—not his Instagram page or his Twitter account, or even his costumes.

In the case of Robbie, being interested in his songs is not easy, already because they are very numerous, much more so than we think. If we examine his musical catalogue, there are more than 300 original songs, more than eighty covers, tracks existing only live, remixes, as well as more than 150 unreleased songs, the latter still sleeping in the drawers.

When I decided to write this book, I asked myself: was I going to talk about ALL the songs? Did I have to be exhaustive? I very quickly discarded the remixes, of course. While remixes may appeal to part of the public as well as myself, they are only a new version of a song that already exists. Why then speak of a remix when we have already mentioned or commented on the original version of the song? Moreover, what is the point of talking about a remix of 'Rock DJ', since this remix is not produced by the singer himself, but by a DJ. Indeed, this book is above all dedicated to Robbie.

Then, the question of unreleased songs arose. Some organisations such as ASCAP (American Society of Composers, Authors, and Publishers) or BMI (Broadcast Music,

Inc.) list all the songs written and/or performed by a singer, whether they have already been published or not. In the case of Robbie, there are about 150 unreleased tracks. But these unreleased tracks raise two issues. On one hand, it is impossible to list them precisely and exhaustively. Indeed, some songs may actually be alternate names of previously released (or even unreleased) songs. For example, what tells us that the unreleased track 'Psychic' is not an alternate name for another unreleased song, 'Psychotic Reaction'? Moreover, very often we do not know anything about these songs, precisely because they are unreleased: what is the song about? Is it a ballad or a dance track? What is the musical style of the song? What are the lyrics like? So many questions that are almost impossible to answer. Sometimes, all the same, we have the approximate date of composition, and most of the time, we also have the names of the composers who collaborated on its creation.

Then comes the case of covers. Robbie has recorded about eighty-five covers. Since these are covers, Robbie is not the author of these songs, and he only put his voice on a melody and lyrics already written. As a result, one might think that they are not really of interest from an artistic point of view: if Robbie composed neither the lyrics nor the melody, we cannot really speak of them as his songs. But what about covers like 'Somethin' Stupid' and 'She's the One'? Both songs are certainly covers, but they both ranked No. 1 in the UK Singles Chart, thus becoming almost his songs though he is not the author. So I decided to comment in the book on some of the covers he recorded, because you cannot ignore them.

Finally, of course, there remains the biggest piece: more than 300 original tracks, recorded and written by Robbie (some written exclusively by Robbie, and most with the help of one or more composers). We are far from the handful of hits that I mentioned above. Who among the audience can name even fifty of them?

This book is therefore mainly devoted to the original tracks and a few covers. For the original tracks, it seems to me almost impossible to comment/describe each of them, exhaustively on one hand because many of them do not need to be commented on (either because they are too weak, too obscure, or too mysterious), and on the other hand because I do not want to bore the reader. We must admit something: it is almost impossible for a singer not to repeat himself. Some songs look alike (either in instruments or musical style, or in lyrics or even voice), and if those songs look alike, their descriptions may look alike as well. Twenty-five love songs written by the same singer are likely to have a lot of similarities.

So I focused on the major songs: obviously the hits, the singles, some covers, as well as some songs that are of particular interest, because they stand out or have a story.

You can read this book like a novel or like a dictionary, consulting it from time to time. If you are surprised or intrigued by the description of the songs I mention in the book, do not hesitate to listen to them or listen to them again while reading my book. You will be able to form your own opinion, or discover the songs from a new angle. Happy reading everyone!

1

Robbie Williams's Studio Sessions

Everyone knows about the successful collaboration between Robbie and Guy Chambers. Guy has produced so many hits on the singer's albums that you would think he was the only composer to have worked with Robbie, but that is far from being the case. Since the beginning of his solo career, the 'Angels' singer has met many writers, and these encounters have given birth to several albums, singles, or even several tracks still unreleased to this day. I aim to tell the history of these meetings here.

It all started in 1995, when Robbie left Take That. At that time, aged twenty-one, the singer was in the midst of a rebellion. He wanted to leave the world of Take That in which he felt imprisoned and took his emancipation. This desire for freedom quickly materialised in June 1995, when Robbie got closer to the band Oasis, one of the most fashionable rock bands of the time. He sympathised with Liam and Noel Gallagher, with whom he played football. There were a series of photos taken at the Glastonbury festival, where the three men are seen together. Robbie even made a short appearance on stage during one of the Oasis concerts at Glastonbury.

On this occasion, Robbie met Owen Morris and Chris Abbot. Owen is none other than the producer of Oasis. Robbie then hung out in the studio with the Gallagher brothers, Owen Morris and Chris Abbot. According to rumours, he provided the backing vocals on the cover of the song 'Cum On Feel the Noize' by the band Slade, but this has never been confirmed.

In the studio, Robbie wrote (or recorded) eleven tracks with Owen Morris and Chris Abbot. Here is the list of songs composed: 'Anthem', 'Cheap Love Song', 'I Should Know Better', 'Lest We Forget', 'Lonely Times', 'Mother', 'Ordinary Days', 'Self Promotion Society', 'Shoo Bee Doo', 'Track 8', and 'Unfinished Business'. Only the track 'Cheap Love Song' saw the light of day: the song appeared on the B-side of the 'South of the Border' single in 1997.

But the friendship between Liam Gallagher was cut short a few years later when Nicole Appleton, Robbie's ex-girlfriend, ended up dating Liam Gallagher (before marrying him). Since that time, Robbie and Liam have become rock's worst enemies.

In 1996, Robbie then met Antony Genn, former musician of the band Pulp, when he became his roommate. Their collaboration started with the single 'Freedom', for which Antony produced the remix 'The Next Big Genn Mix'.

While Robbie thought about recording his first solo album, Antony lent him a hand, and together, they wrote several tracks: 'Clean', 'Summertime', 'I Can Play', 'It's Not Me', 'Stop the World', 'Sunny Vision', and 'What's It Gonna Take', yet only the songs 'Clean' and 'Summertime' saw the light of day (the former is found on the album *Life thru a Lens*, while the latter is reused several times by the singer: first on the soundtrack of the film *Mike Bassett: England Manager* then on the album *Rudebox*, where it is offered in a more electro version).

The following year, in 1997, Robbie met Desmond Child, with whom he recorded the song 'Old Before I Die', which would become one of the singles from his album *Life thru a Lens*. The two men recorded two other tracks at this time: 'Almost Perfect' and 'I Wish I Didn't Care'. They remain unreleased to this day.

Then came Guy Chambers, and the famous meeting changed Robbie's fate forever. When Robbie met Guy Chambers, he was still plagued by his demons: alcohol and drugs. It was Guy who helped Robbie to get past these. Together, they wrote and produced a series of songs that later became classics: for the first album, *Life thru a Lens*, they composed 'Angels', 'Let Me Entertain You', 'Lazy Days', and 'South of the Border'.

The recording of the album *Life thru a Lens* was done exclusively in the studios of Maison Rouge LTD in March 1997. Suffice to say, the recording session for this album was the shortest and most profitable for the singer.

The following year, in 1998, Robbie returned to the studio with Guy Chambers to work on his second album: *I've Been Expecting You*. While *Life thru a Lens* had been produced in a single studio, this time the singer and his mentor utilised several studios such as Wheeler End, Jacobs Studios, Angel Recording Studios, and even the legendary Abbey Road Studios. Other hits were born there: 'Millennium', 'Strong', 'No Regrets', and 'She's the One'.

It is also necessary to underline other collaborations, some quite well known and others totally ignored by the public. For example, there was a short collaboration with his girlfriend at the time, Nicole Appleton, and with her they wrote 'Love Is Where I'm From', which is still unreleased today.

In 2000, after the monstrous successes of *Life thru a Lens* and *I've Been Expecting You*, Williams and Chambers became famous in the pop/rock universe and it was not long before this magical duo obtained the interest of other personalities, such as Australian singer Kylie Minogue, who was making her musical comeback, and any precious help was therefore more than welcome. Robbie, Kylie, and Guy then recorded 'Kids', which later became one of the singer's biggest hits. At the same time, the three artists also recorded the songs 'Loveboat' and 'Your Disco Needs You'. Finally, another track written by this trio is born: 'My Song', but this one is still unpublished to this day.

These recordings with the Australian singer are added to those of the album *Sing When You're Winning*. Once again, Guy Chambers and Robbie worked together to the delight of fans, and a new delivery of hits took place: 'Rock DJ', 'Let Love Be

Your Energy', 'Supreme', 'The Road to Mandalay', and 'Better Man'. This time, the recording sessions mostly took place at Master Rock Studios and Sarm Hook End.

From 2001, Robbie began to frequent Hollywood. In search of novelty, he approached several rock stars, such as Brian May or Billy Morrison. Since the death of Freddie Mercury in 1991, the band Queen had been looking for a future, and the idea of replacing Freddie with a new singer was slowly gaining ground. The band then planned to recruit Robbie. After all, he had the profile: a sexy young man, with a sulphurous and provocative attitude, virile, and possessing a voice capable of rubbing shoulders with both bass and treble. It was in this context that Robbie recorded with the band's guitarist, Brian May, a cover of the song 'We Are the Champions', which was used for the soundtrack of the film *A Knight's Tale*. In the music video shot for the occasion, we see another key musician: Billy Morrison. Robbie and Billy then compose together the track 'Coffee, Tea & Sympathy', which later appears on the single of 'Something Beautiful'.

The collaboration with Brian May was not limited to the cover of 'We Are the Champions'. The guitarist also appears on the track 'Eternity', for which he provides a guitar solo. With Robbie, he also wrote a song: 'Say It Ain't True', which Brian later used at several charity concerts.

In August 2001, as Robbie completed his new European tour, he immediately returned to Los Angeles to record his fourth solo album: *Swing When You're Winning*. For this album of swing covers, he essentially locked himself away in the famous Capitol Studios in Los Angeles. Surrounded by an orchestra, the singer put his voice to great classics of swing, as well as the original composition, 'I Will Talk and Hollywood Will Listen'.

Each year corresponds to a new meeting. In 2002, while Robbie was busy recording his new album, which was later titled *Escapology*, he met Boots Ottestad and Ashley Hamilton. With them, he recorded the song 'Come Undone'. This song, which became one of the hits of his new album, was the subject of the falling out between Guy Chambers and the singer. Indeed, Guy said at the time that if 'Come Undone' was released as a single, then he would refuse to play it live.

With Boots Ottestad and Ashley Hamilton, Robbie wrote several tracks: 'Boots Tripping', 'Come Undone', 'Communication Breakdown', 'Vegas', and 'Wimmin''.

Only 'Come Undone' saw the light of day in Robbie's discography. 'Wimmin'', meanwhile, was born on an Ashley single.

Other songs were recorded with Boots and Robbie (but without Ashley): 'Do Me Now' (present on the single 'Misunderstood'), and 'Hey Wow Yeah Yeah', on the album *Take the Crown*. The other songs written by Boots and Robbie ('Get a Life', 'Goin' Down', 'I Love You All', 'I Love You More Than I Like You Now', 'Psychic', and 'Vegas') are still unreleased to this day.

When 2003 arrived, Guy Chambers jumped ship. Following an essentially financial quarrel in October 2002 (during the signing of the new deal between Robbie and EMI Music), Guy and Robbie separated.

The 'Feel' singer had to find a new partner, and this came about during the summer of 2003, while he was on tour. He crossed the path of Stephen Duffy, and their collaboration began immediately. However, this was not their first meeting. Later, Stephen confessed that they first met in 1996, on the *Top of the Pops* TV show; Duffy recalled:

> I first met Rob at *T.O.T.P.* when I appeared with Me Me Me and he was at number two with 'Freedom'. I worked with Claire Worrall in the Lilac Time, and she then also joined Rob's band, and she kept passing my records to Rob and he liked them. That is where we got our musical relationship.

The two artists first wrote together a series of unreleased tracks which were used for the *Greatest Hits*, released in 2004. In addition to 'Radio' and 'Misunderstood', several unreleased tracks produced by this new couple made their appearance as B-sides of these two singles.

Success is there: 'Radio' ranked No. 1 in singles sales and then became an encouraging sign to extend this particularly fruitful collaboration. In 2005, they recorded the album *Intensive Care* together; following the album's release, in 2006 Robbie performed what was his biggest world tour.

When 'Radio' was released, Duffy said:

> Radio was released today. This is the new single from Robbie Williams, and I'm proud to be the co-composer and co-producer of it. It was composed in my old studios at Air Studios. This song, and most new songs written with Robbie are written in improvisation with sounds, beats, and jamming with Robbie. It's a way of working that neither of us had tried before. Radio is now taking a new direction now that we are playing it live. Therefore, the experimentation continues, and there is no need to release the album before spring 2005. It's very exciting and I feel very lucky.

At the same time, other writers were appearing and came back to sprinkle the singer's musical catalogue on several occasions. This is particularly the case of the writer Chris Heath. He was first involved in the writing of the book *Feel* by Robbie in 2004, then in that of songs like 'Sin Sin Sin', 'Make Me Pure', and 'King of Bloke and Bird', which were integrated into the album *Intensive Care*.

But their collaboration does not stop there. There are new contributions from Chris on the track 'Keep On' from the album *Rudebox*, as well as on the albums *Swings Both Ways* and *The Heavy Entertainment Show*.

One of the most mysterious recordings was that of the album *Rudebox*. Indeed, we do not know when exactly this album was recorded. While 2005 was devoted to the recording of *Intensive Care*, 2006 was essentially dedicated to the Close Encounters Tour. As a result, when the *Rudebox* album was released in October

2006, fans were amazed: how could he find the time to record these seventeen new tracks?

Anyway, this album brings together many producers, and this is the second surprise. While all his previous albums were produced by a single producer (Guy Chambers or Stephen Duffy), *Rudebox* brings together a host of artists, such as Soul Mekanik, Mark Ronson, The Pet Shop Boys, and William Orbit, to name a few.

This is the opportunity for us to discuss the importance of the band Soul Mekanik in the career of the singer. This band, originally from Stoke-on-Trent, Robbie's hometown, is made up of two musician brothers: Daniel Spencer Mould and Kevin Andrews Mould. Over the years, they have been among Robbie's most loyal collaborators. Specialising in electro, they also use their talents for some of the singer's swing tracks.

Their collaboration began in 2000, on the album *Sing When You're Winning*. Together they wrote the tracks 'Rock DJ', 'Knutsford City Limits', and 'Love Calling Earth'. They are also the authors of the song 'Dance With the Devil', a song which appears only on the *Where Egos Dare* DVD.

In 2006, the friends met to work on the *Rudebox* album. They wrote 'Rudebox', 'Burslem Normals', and 'Viva Life on Mars'. They also made many remixes under the name of their band Soul Mekanik.

In 2009, they wrote most of the tracks on the album *Reality Killed the Video Star*: 'You Know Me', 'Morning Sun', 'Somewhere', and 'Won't Do That'.

Again in 2012, the two natives of Stoke-on-Trent wrote the songs 'On My Own' and 'Soul Transmission' for the *Different* EP.

Another musician regularly intervenes in Robbie's career: Jerry Meehan, the bassist of his band. At the time of recording *Rudebox*, he was the author of several tracks, such as 'The 80's', 'The 90's', 'Dickhead', and 'Good Doctor'. One of his songs also remained in the drawers for a long time before finally being unveiled: the song 'Love Is You' finally found its place in 2014 on the album *Under the Radar—Volume 1*. Finally, he collaborated in the writing of two other songs: 'Sean Connery (Love Cats)' and 'Two Big Poofs', which are still unreleased today.

When Robbie returned to the studio in 2009 after a three-year absence, he surrounded himself this time with Trevor Horn for the production of his new album, *Reality Killed the Video Star*, the title being a nod to Trevor's greatest hit, 'Video Killed the Radio Star'. Stephen Duffy was no longer in the picture. The writing, on the other hand, is not provided by Trevor Horn, but by Soul Mekanik.

After a short detour to Take That in 2010, Robbie then thought of recording an album of duets with his oldest collaborator: Gary Barlow. Together, they notably wrote 'Candy' and 'Different', two songs later released as singles. Meanwhile, Robbie met two Australians: Flynn Francis and Tim Metcalfe, also known as the Undercolours. Seduced by this umpteenth meeting, Robbie cancelled his duet project with Gary Barlow and locked himself in the studio with the Australian duo for the recording of *Take the Crown*. The production is entrusted to Jacknife Lee.

That was when the incredible happened. While Guy Chambers and Robbie had been angry with each other for ten years, they end up reconciling at the end of 2012 during concerts given at the O2 in London. From there to returning to the studio, there was only one step, which they took in January 2013, to record the singer's new swing album: *Swings Both Ways*. Guy Chambers then took full control, taking care of both studio production and production on tour. Of course, he continued to help Robbie writing new songs.

Flynn Francis and Tim Metcalfe were not ousted for all that. For the Take the Crown tour, they were present and also participated in the recording of *Under the Radar*, as well as that of *The Heavy Entertainment Show*. In fact, since the *Rudebox* album, it was no longer an exclusive songwriter who accompanied Robbie (Guy Chambers or Stephen Duffy), but a large family of composers/producers, where the roles were not frozen—some took part in the writing as well as production.

Moreover, *The Heavy Entertainment Show* and *The Christmas Present* sound almost like a compendium of artists who have already worked with Robbie in the past.

To sum up, the history of the recording sessions of Robbie's albums is particularly interesting. Over the years, the meetings having multiplied, with the singer going from exclusive collaborations to increasingly diversified collaborations, involving more and more artists. This richness is also reflected in the different musical styles that Robbie has tried: first naturally attracted by Brit Pop between 1995 and 2000, he expanded his musical catalogue by moving towards swing in 2001, then rap and electro in 2006 with *Rudebox*. Seduced by a more retro style while working with Trevor Horn in 2009, he then devoted himself to pure and hard rock from the album *Take the Crown*, without forgetting his musical roots: pop rock and swing.

What is arguably most amazing is the ease and spontaneity with which Robbie enters the studio. Most often, a simple meeting, during a TV show, a concert, or an evening, gives birth to an immediate collaboration or featuring. Songs written or recorded with artists such as Tom Jones, Rod Stewart, Dizzee Rascal, Big Narstie, Bob Sinclar, Emma Bunton, Ronan Keating, or The Struts have often been triggered by pure chance. The number of collaborations with other artists is so great that it sometimes feels like Robbie walks into the studio every time he says 'hello'.

2

Life thru a Lens

Release date:	29 September 1997
Writers:	Robbie Williams, Guy Chambers, Desmond Child, Eric Brazilian, Antony Genn, Martin Slattery, Richard Hawley
Producers:	Guy Chambers, Steve Power
Studios:	Matrix Maison Rouge LTD
Recordings:	October 1996–March 1997
Duration:	52:46
Label:	Chrysalis/EMI

The album *Life thru a Lens* was Robbie's first solo album after his breakup with Take That in 1995 and his first solo single 'Freedom', released in 1996. While the album was recorded between October 1996 and March 1997, the first single, 'Old Before I Die', came out the following month! The singer released two more singles in July and September, before finally releasing the album on 29 September 1997. But sales of the album did not really take off until Christmas 1997, after the release of the biggest hit of his career, 'Angels', on 1 December. Finally, a last single ended the exploitation of the album in March of the following year: 'Let Me Entertain You'. If we had to retain a single musical influence on this album, it would be that of the band Oasis, which is no surprise when you consider that Robbie spent whole days with them in 1995. In 2022, the album was reissued; several unreleased demos and two unreleased tracks ('Hey Little Girl' and 'Red Lights') were incorporated in this reissue.

'Lazy Days'

Writers:	Robbie Williams, Guy Chambers
Duration:	3:54
Single release date:	14 July 1997
Charts:	No. 8 in UK

The album opens with a particularly rock-heavy track: 'Lazy Days'. The intro of percussion and guitar corresponds perfectly to what one expects from a rock song of the '90s. The song has a little 'Oasis feeling', which was very fashionable at the time.

The lyrics curiously echo those of his hit 'Angels'. In 'Lazy Days', he sings: 'We don't need any reason/To sit around and wait', while his track 'Angels' begins with 'I sit and wait'.

'Lazy Days' was written by Guy Chambers when he was part of the Lemon Trees band. Robbie later changed the lyrics and music before incorporating it into his album.

'Life thru a Lens'

Writers: Robbie Williams, Guy Chambers
Duration: 3:07

This track evokes his relationship with Tara Palmer-Tomkison, with whom he was romantically linked at the time.

This is the perfect song to start the day, not just for the lyrics—the line 'Wake up on Sunday morning' opens the track—but also for the dynamism and energy that emerges from the first seconds. This track is a treat, and we do not understand why it was not released as a single. On the lyrics front, Robbie rhymes at a frantic pace, and the words are as punchy as the percussion of his drummer.

The track ends with an exhilarating acceleration that suggests great moments to come on the album!

'Ego a Go Go'

Writers: Robbie Williams, Guy Chambers
Duration: 3:34

'Angels'

Writers: Robbie Williams, Guy Chambers
Duration: 4:25
Single release date: 1 December 1997
Charts: No. 4 in UK
Sales: 1.8 million copies in UK

According to Robbie, 'Angels' was one of the very first songs he wrote with Guy Chambers. But the very first version of Robbie's famous hit is said to have been written by Irish composer Ray Heffernan in Paris in 1996. Heffernan then showed this version to Robbie in Dublin. Although the Irish composer was behind the very first demo of the track, the final version comes from the work of Robbie and Guy Chambers.

This track, which strangely enough has never been No. 1 in charts, has met a very special fate. When we think of 'Angels', we first think of a ballad, a beautiful love song that overwhelms the hearts of young women. But this song is much more complex. The song begins on a piano which enforces its incredible strength, very quickly supported by the voice of Robbie that comes to rest there. Then come the violins, the guitar, and the choirs, which reinforce the power of the melody.

The key to the track is there: strength and simplicity. The song unfolds like a prayer. First, the singer's voice and his calm provide a solemn feeling to the song. The audience feels compelled to listen carefully to what he has to say to us. Second, musically, 'Angels' is not a pop song. We are moving more towards a ballad on very classic instruments: piano and violins. The presence of the choirs also reinforces this dimension.

This 'prayer' really takes off in the accompanying music video: filmed in black and white, the style is particularly neat, as neat as an advertisement for a branded perfume.

But let us come back to the details: we have in front of us a man entirely dressed in black (a turtleneck sweater, a long coat, and gloves), like a priest saying his prayers. Unconsciously, this very fashionable outfit refers to the religious theme. Respect and elegance are reflected in the video. A helicopter strangely passes through the sky, like a modern-day angel. The only disturbing elements are the presence of the football and the motorbike, which would later become recurring objects in the singer's imagery.

This is undoubtedly where the song draws its success; it is not only in the romanticism of the lyrics, but, above all, in all the religious symbolism of the song: a man, Robbie, who expresses with strength and elegance, his convictions and beliefs. He talks about angels, about love and being loved.

Therefore, it is no wonder the song has become an anthem over the years. In concert, the track is sung almost systematically, always towards the end of the show, and obviously everyone knows the lyrics by heart. At religious events, it is often played at funerals and weddings. Finally, the song has grown to such an extent that it is even regularly sung at the end of football matches in the UK.

'South of the Border'

Writers:	Robbie Williams, Guy Chambers
Duration:	3:53
Single release date:	15 September 1997
Charts:	No. 14 in UK

The music video takes place in a house on fire, but we feel that the presence of the fire is undoubtedly an allegory to evoke the dangers of drugs.

Robbie sings 'But I toe the line', a line he later repeats in another song on the album, 'Clean'. Above all, interestingly, he goes on to add: '... and move the time to a town called No Regrets'. We guess then that the famous track 'No Regrets' was probably already written at the time when 'South of the Border' was recorded.

Otherwise, this is a delicious rock song that speaks of Kate Moss, and which is ideal to be sung in concert.

'Old Before I Die'

Writers:	Desmond Child, Eric Brazilian
Duration:	3:53
Single release date:	14 April 1997
Charts:	No. 2 in UK, No. 1 in Spain

If you want to hear what Robbie's voice sounded like early on in his solo career, 'Old Before I Die' is just right. We can clearly see his pretty little voice of a typically English young man.

Speaking of age, it is the theme of the song. 'I hope I'm old before I die' he repeats in the track. Just like in the song 'Let Me Entertain You', where we heard a little French with '*Mon cher*', another French expression makes its appearance here: '*C'est la vie* I say'.

This track is a response to The Who's 'My Generation', in which you can hear 'I hope I die before I get old'. Robbie reversed the words to respond, 'I hope I'm old before I die'.

In 2002, at a private concert, Robbie performed 'My Generation' with the band Camp Freddy.

'One of God's Better People'

Writers:	Robbie Williams, Guy Chambers
Duration:	3:33

'Let Me Entertain You'

Writers:	Robbie Williams, Guy Chambers
Duration:	4:22
Single release date:	16 March 1998
Charts:	No. 3 in UK

This track is not just a song, but the official opening credits for Robbie Williams's concerts. When the first notes of this thunderous track hit live, fans realise that the show is on and that they will have a great time with the 'King of Entertainment' because entertainment, partying, fun, and delirium is what it is all about. This is the song of all excess: no room for moderation!

'Hell', 'ass', 'scream', 'die', 'burning'—these are some of the words that are mentioned in the lyrics, and the stage is set very quickly. Everything is done here to excite the public: rock music, a booming piano, dry and frenzied guitar riffs, frenzied percussions, and certain effects which sound like alarms. In other words, it is almost impossible to stay calm while listening to this song! The repetition of the famous 'Come on, come on, come on, come on' encourages the audience to let go, to jump and scream.

If we watch the music video, the excitement will only be heightened: Robbie wears makeup similar to that of the band Kiss, proudly showing off his manly and hairy chest, surrounded by his very rock-like band and sexy girls which seems to come straight from a crazy version of George Michael's 'Freedom' music video.

'Let Me Entertain You' sounds like a dynamic call to party and hysteria. Starting a concert this way is a way to tease the audience and give a taste of what will be next!

Robbie and Guy Chambers are said to have been inspired by the Rolling Stones movie *Rock and Roll Circus*.

'Killing Me'

Writers: Robbie Williams, Guy Chambers
Duration: 3:56

'Clean'

Writers: Antony Genn, Martin Slattery, Richard Hawley
Duration: 3:55

Another pretty happy song (it was probably better, after the sad break with Take That), and the track title alone calls out to us: 'Clean'. When you know Robbie's drug problems back then, you can guess what the song is about!

The opening lines of the song confirm the theme: 'There was a time/When crazy days would start with wine/And now I tow a different line'. One can hardly be more explicit. The singer also mentions 'Mr. Sheen' to talk about Charlie Sheen, who also had some troubles with drugs.

While 'Ego a Go Go' was a celebration of his breakup with Take That, 'Clean' sounds like a (temporary) release from his drug addiction.

'Baby Girl Window'

Writers: Robbie Williams, Guy Chambers
Duration: 3:16

'Hello Sir'

Writers: Robbie Williams
Duration: 1:26

With the tradition of hidden tracks on albums becoming all the rage in the '90s, Robbie's first contribution to the trend was 'Hello Sir'.

'Hello Sir' is not really a song, but more of a poem. It is also the shortest track on the album. 'Hello Sir' has become, over the years, one of the tracks that the fans prefer, for the sincerity which seems to emerge from this text. Accompanied by a very discreet piano, Robbie speaks here to one of his former teachers. In a provocative tone, the singer seems to want revenge on him: 'Hello sir, remember me?/I'm the man you thought I'd never be/The boy who you reduced to tears'. And the least we can say is that it is not neutral: 'For the negative dickheads just like you'.

For this album devoted to the theme of celebrity, Robbie has therefore chosen to end it with this vengeful poem, thus affirming his victory: he is not the loser that this famous professor tried to make believe; on the contrary, he has became a famous celebrity known all over the world.

B-sides linked to *Life thru a Lens*

'Average' B-Side

Writers: Robbie Williams, Kevin King
Duration: 2:58
B-side of the single 'Old Before I Die'

Another song where Robbie is mainly accompanied by a guitar. Charming song, but which, as its name suggests, is quite 'average'.

'Better Days'

Writers: Robbie Williams, Guy Chambers
Duration: 3:00
B-side of the single 'Old Before I Die'

Song with typical Britpop sounds, with a strong presence of choirs and percussion.

'Kooks'

Writers: David Bowie
Duration: 3:00
B-side of the single 'Old Before I Die'

'Making Plans for Nigel'

Writers: Colin Moulding
Duration: 4:05
B-side of the single 'Old Before I Die'

This song is a cover, but it is certainly addressed to Nigel Martin-Smith, the former manager of Take That, with whom Robbie was in a legal battle at one time. That said, given the simplicity of the lyrics, it is very difficult to make the connection between the Nigel of the song and the manager of Take That.

'Teenage Millionaire'

Writers: Robbie Williams, Guy Chambers, Chris Sharrock
Duration: 3:09
B-side of the single 'Lazy Days'

If we had to choose only one song to best describe Robbie's state of mind in the years 1996–98, we would certainly choose this track, 'Teenage Millionaire'. Why?

Because this song exudes rebellion and arrogance, two notions that characterise the beginning of the singer's solo career. Just separated from Take That, Robbie had only one goal: to free himself from his past and convince the public that he would become a huge star. We find this state of mind in several songs recorded at this time, such as 'Let Me Entertain You', 'Karma Killer', or 'It's Only Us'.

The song begins with an interview, in which a journalist asks Robbie about his past. We understand that she is talking about the band Take That. Robbie begins a response, before moving on to the song itself. The style of this one is voluntarily rock and the lyrics abundantly describe its sulphurous past.

He sings 'Riding in your limos/Hanging with your bimbos' and 'Coke and whisky chasers/I ain't supposed to pose/But I don't care'. We understand through the lines that Robbie sums up his Take That period with the excesses that resulted from it: excess of all kinds, and easy money.

Failing to end up on the album, the song still ended up on the Japanese version of *Life thru a Lens*.

'Falling In Bed (Again)'

Writers: Robbie Williams, Matt Hay
Duration: 3:28
B-side of the single 'Lazy Days'

Robbie recounts here a brief romantic encounter. The song ends like the end of a failed joke.

'She Makes Me High'

Writers: Robbie Williams, Guy Chambers, Gary Nuttall
Duration: 3:24
B-side of the single 'Lay Days'

This song might have deserved to appear on the album *Life thru a Lens*. Dynamic, supported by a simple but effective chorus and very present choirs, 'She Makes Me High' has it all!

'Evr'y Time We Say Goodbye'

Writers: Cole Porter
Duration: 3:03
B-side of the single 'Lazy Days'

Recorded as the B-side of the single 'Lazy Days', 'Evr'y Time We Say Goodbye' is arguably the singer's first swing experience. This is a Cole Porter cover—an artist that Robbie will resume again ten years later, in 2007, during the release of the tribute album, *Forever Cool*. Accompanied only by a piano, Robbie seizes the opportunity here to highlight his charming voice, one of his main assets.

'Cheap Love Song'

Writers: Robbie Williams, Owen Morris, Chris Abbot
Duration: 4:10
B-side of the single 'South of the Border'

We recognise here the style of the *Life thru a Lens* album: simple lyrics and a certain lightness. The title of the song also defines very well what it is about here: a cheap love song!

'Walk This Sleigh'

Writers: Robbie Williams, Guy Chambers
Duration: 3:01
B-side of the single 'Angels'

Twenty-two years before *The Christmas Present*, Robbie released a rather unusual Christmas song, titled 'Walk This Sleigh' as a B-side alongside the famous 'Angels' single in December 1997.

The lyrics are quite funny. After a first verse where the singer makes several more or less implicit religious references, he then moves on to much more simplistic and repetitive lyrics.

The irony of fate (unless this title inspired Robbie afterwards) is that the lyrics of this song contain two titles of songs that Robbie will sing in 2019. He sings 'Roastin' oats on open fires', which refers to the famous Christmas song, 'Chestnuts Roasting on an Open Fire', a song he covers in 2019 on the album *The Christmas Present*.

Similarly, the lyrics also contain this line: 'Happy birthday Jesus Christ'. This phrase would became the name of a song written by Robbie, also on his album *The Christmas Present*.

'Get the Joke'

Writers: Robbie Williams, Gary Nuttall
Duration: 3:03
B-side of the single 'Angels'

Listening to this song, it feels like all Robbie was trying to do while writing this track was find good rhymes! This nice song, rather pleasant, has no other interest. Note, however, that it was composed with Gary Nuttall. Gary will subsequently become the only member of the band to have accompanied Robbie from his debut to the present day!

'Karaoke Overkill'

Writers: Robbie Williams, Guy Chambers
Duration: 3:00
B-side of the single 'Angels'

'I Wouldn't Normally Do This Kind of Thing'

Writers: Neil Tennant, Chris Lowe
Duration: 3:06
B-side of the single 'Angels'

Robbie uses a song from the Pet Shop Boys here. This is undoubtedly the first wink given to the Pet Shop Boys before collaborating with them afterwards ('No Regrets' a few months later, then 'She's Madonna', 'Jealousy', etc.).

We note that Robbie sings mainly in the treble to take up the effeminate voice of the British duo.

'I'm the Reserection'

Writers: Robbie Williams, Guy Chambers
Duration: 3:48
B-side of the single 'Let Me Entertain You'

When we know Robbie's bad boy humour, we are not too surprised by the nice pun that Robbie slips into the title of this song, 'I'm the Reserection'! Once past the smile stage, we enjoy discovering this B-side which alternates quiet verses and rock choruses. Robbie lists here a series of celebrities, among which we find mainly women: Yoko Ono, Mia Farrow, and Shirley Bassey. The end of the song is a loud and joyful climax, like an orgasm.

'Hey Little Girl'

Writers: Richard Hawley
Duration: 4:05
Track revealed on the 2022 *Life Thru a Lens* edition

This demo was recorded in October or November 1996.

'Red Lights'

Writers: Robbie Williams, Guy Chambers
Duration: 2:58
Track revealed on the 2022 *Life Thru a Lens* edition

This demo was recorded in January 1997.

3

I’ve Been Expecting You

Release date:	26 October 1998
Writers:	Robbie Williams, Guy Chambers, Leslie Bricusse, John Barry, Loudon Wainwright III, Karl Wallinger, Fil Eisler
Producers:	Guy Chambers, Steve Power
Studios:	Trident Studios, Wheeler End, Swanyard Studios, Blah Street, Jacobs Studios, Angel Recording Studios, Abbey Road Studio
Recordings:	1998
Duration:	76:02 (1998)/75:14 (since 2002)
Label:	Chrysalis/EMI

It is often said that a singer’s second album is the most important one, and *I’ve Been Expecting You* is no exception. After the huge success of the single ‘Angels’, the media were waiting to see what Robbie would produce next with bated breath. He clearly had no room for error, and we can say that the singer wins the challenge hands down! Driven by the success of the single ‘Millennium’ (his first No. 1 in sales), the album ranked directly at No. 1 in sales upon release. Four more singles followed, three of which would become classics in the singer’s career: ‘No Regrets’, ‘Strong’, ‘She’s the One’ (also No. 1), and ‘Win Some Lose Some’ for the Australian market. *I’ve Been Expecting You* looks like the sketch of the typical Britpop album from the late ’90s. It features the ingredients that Robbie handles best: humour, love, glitter, arrogance, and rock! After the celebrity theme in *Life thru a Lens*, Robbie chooses James Bond’s theme here: funny and sexy imagery permeates the album. It is found both in the songs of the album, in the artwork, and even in three music videos from this new opus!

‘Strong’

Writers:	Robbie Williams, Guy Chambers
Duration:	4:39
Single release date:	15 March 1999
Charts:	No. 4 in UK

Robbie wrote 'Strong' in a hotel in Cologne, Germany. The song was inspired by his fans, who follow him to the hotel doors. In concert, the singer has developed the habit, since 2003, of transforming the song into a karaoke session; the lyrics are then displayed on a giant screen, and the public is invited to sing the lyrics at the top of their lungs!

While one would expect this second album to kick off with a powerful track to assert your ego, Robbie decides otherwise. The song 'Strong' is misleading; it does not highlight its strengths, but on the contrary its weaknesses: 'You think that I'm strong/You're wrong'.

'Strong' is also written with a lot of skill. The lyrics echo the first album, and thus make it possible to make the connection with the new album that this opens. He sings in particular: 'I look like Kiss but without the make-up', referring to the 'Let Me Entertain You' music video in which Robbie is made up as the singer of the band Kiss. 'So before I'm old I'll confess' may refer to the single 'Old Before I Die' from the previous album.

The most ironic fate is reserved for the music video. While Robbie once again faced his demons in March 1999, struggling with substance abuse, the record company decided to release precisely this single in which Robbie claims that he is not strong. In fact, EMI had to use archival footage to make the video as the singer himself was unable to shoot one.

'No Regrets'

Writers:	Robbie Williams, Guy Chambers
Duration:	5:11
Single release date:	30 November 1998
Charts:	No. 4 in UK

What a gem! This song gives me so many thrills and emotions. There is so much to say about the track; it is as if angels, a fairy, and a magician have come together to create one of the most beautiful pop songs of the '90s.

The first seconds start a bit like a lullaby with pop sounds that end in a dream! Then comes Robbie's sweet voice, with the same delicacy as that of the track 'Angels'. If the previous song could be summed up in 'no force', this one tells us 'no regrets'. After evoking his demons in the first track, Robbie dedicates the song here to his breakup with Take That.

After a long lyrical introduction that ends with 'So I softly slip away', the song slowly slips towards a rise in power both lyrical and instrumental with the arrival of the chorus: 'No regrets they don't work/No regrets they only hurt'. And who then comes in the choirs? The talented Neil Tennant of the Pet Shop Boys, whose famous feminine voice resembles that of an angel; this voice is almost as important as Robbie's in this song!

After a successful instrumental bridge, the dramatisation of the lyrics begins to emerge: 'I don't want to hate/But that's all you've left me with'. Then Robbie's anger grows, before letting another guest joining the chorus: Neil Hannon from the band Divine Comedy, another very popular artist in 1998. His arrival is more subtle than that of the leader of the Pet Shop Boys. If Neil Tennant sings like an angel, Neil Hannon's dark voice resonates like that of a demon. And in the middle, the bitterness of the singer of 'Angels', trapped and torn between the voices of his two acolytes, reaches its climax in the following verse: 'Remember the photographs insane/The ones where we all laugh so lame/We were having the time of our lives/Well thank you, it was a real blast'. Neil Hannon then takes over, performing his own version of the chorus solo in a much more melancholy style: 'No regrets, they don't work/No regrets, they only hurt'.

The song ends with a 'spoken word recited' by Robbie, in which he judges and condemns the other person with a series of scathing, blood-curdling sentences. Here is the end, with a final stab: 'I guess the love we once had/Is officially/Dead!'

And what about the accompanying music video! The singer, dressed in an elegant grey suit, leaves a glamorous film studio to walk through several paths (a single road, a freeway, and in town), as if he wanted to stage a flight forward. Desperate (or suicidal), the singer stops to fill a canister with gasoline. But he then starts to flee (the flight representing regret) and when the leak catches fire, it ends up catching up with Robbie dramatically at the very end of the video, who stops abruptly when the flame reaches him and that he pronounces the word 'Dead'.

The video was also censored: the image of the truck that nearly crushed Robbie on the highway was removed, presumably at the request of Road Safety who deemed that this image promoted risky behaviour.

The song is not just about his breakup with Take That. It can be interpreted as a text about the end of a romantic relationship.

'Millennium'

Writers:	Robbie Williams, Guy Chambers, Leslie Bricusse, John Barry
Duration:	4:07
Single release date:	7 September 1998
Charts:	No. 1 in UK

It was when I discovered the 'Millennium' music video in September 1998 that I became a fan: seeing on the screen a handsome kid performing a series of funny and sexy faces and winks (no less than five winks in the video) literally won me over. I had not felt such a thrill of excitement since Madonna's 'Erotica' music video in October 1992. The gold glitter from the 'Millennium' music video echoed the black and sulphurous glitter from Madonna's music video. Robbie wears a black James Bond-type suit, while Madonna sports a tight black dress that any James Bond girl could wear. In five winks, the parallelism between the two videos was established, and my admiration for Robbie sealed forever.

Aged twenty-four at the time, and after the incredible success met with the Take That period and the single 'Angels', it was not inconsistent to propose a video where the singer finds himself surrounded by beautiful young women, in prestigious settings. The idea of the James Bond theme, of which Robbie is a fan, is rather welcome here. The music video was shot in Pinewood Studios, where the James Bond films are shot! The music video refers to several James Bond films: *Thunderball* and *From Russia with Love*.

In fact, all the ingredients are gathered here to compose a hit. First, the choice of the song itself: writing a song called 'Millennium' two years before the highly anticipated year 2000 was already a good choice. We all remember the excitement of the media at the time, as the millennium approached.

Then, there is the musical theme: here, Robbie uses a sample of the song 'You Only Live Twice' by Nancy Sinatra, which served as the main theme in the film of the same name, from the James Bond series. To use this sample (thus avoiding accusations of plagiarism) to give a second life to this track, by keeping the theme of the adventures of the most famous secret agent in the United Kingdom, was a daring but perfectly successful bet, so much that the final result is a matter of mastery and excellence.

A rolling cymbal and the festive 'ouh ouh ouh' which opens the track 'Millennium', accompanied by the sample of 'You Only Live Twice', immediately announce the colour; we are facing a song with flamboyant features. After the excesses already discussed in the 'Let Me Entertain You' music video, we find again the excesses in the lyrics of 'Millennium': 'Live for liposuction/And detox for your rent/Overdose at Christmas/And give it up for Lent'.

Then come several repetitions of the famous chorus starting with 'We've got stars directing our fate', which leave the provocative 'Come and have a go if you think you are hard enough' where we guess, in the background, is the atmosphere of a football stadium, no doubt to amplify the underlying excitement. Further on, he begins a rap debut, with this verse: 'And when we come we always come too late/I often think that we were born to hate/Get up and see the sarcasm in my eyes'.

'Millennium' is so perfect, both in terms of the music video, the melody, and the music, that we almost forget the meaning of the lyrics: they encourage us to enjoy life, even if it means burning it; to live in the excess, because our fate is sealed anyway and our end is inevitable. And this is a bit of the reason why the choice of the title 'Millennium' is rather fitting: the uncertainty being with the approach of the new millennium, as much as to live thoroughly, before the end of the world comes.

'Phoenix from the Flames'

Writers: Robbie Williams, Guy Chambers
Duration: 4:02

When we know the track 'Millennium' well, we understand why 'Phoenix from the Flames' comes just behind. After the flamboyant 'Millennium', we continue here on a track which reveals, little by little, all its power and its greatness.

The song begins with a fairly smooth intro on the piano, and its tone gradually rises, supported by powerful choirs, then loud music, to then descend and return to the starting point. The message is rather optimistic: nothing can stop the singer, and despite the obstacles, the man still manages to get up. Symbolically, 'Phoenix from the Flames' could actually sum up the singer's entire career. In turn, Robbie has had to face his demons, extinguish himself, and then rise from his ashes, like a phoenix, several times in his career.

'Win Some Lose Some'

Writers: Robbie Williams, Guy Chambers
Duration: 4:18
Single release date: 13 March 2000
Charts: No. 7 in New Zealand

The fifth track of the album is arguably the first love song of the opus. It is a celebration of life, and it is believed to be, in keeping with the words of 'Millennium', a celebration of life and an incentive to enjoy happiness. It is also a love song about Nicole Appleton. The singer intervenes at the beginning of the song with her famous 'I love you baby'.

'Grace'

Writers: Robbie Williams, Guy Chambers
Duration: 3:13

Here we completely change the register. We forget the glitter and the show. 'Grace' is a much lighter song, quite retro in style (especially when the 'la la la la' sung by the choirs occur). Listening to the first few seconds, we imagine ourselves on vacation, by the sea, in a rather heavenly setting.

'Jesus in a Camper Van'

Writers: Robbie Williams, Guy Chambers, Loudon Wainwright III
Duration: 3:39

Shortly after the album's release, Robbie was sued over this song. The reason: the track contains lyrics very similar to Woody Guthrie's 1961 song 'I Am the Way' (or Loudon Wainwright III's 1973 version). Indeed, the song 'I Am the Way' contains this sentence: 'Every son of God has a little hard luck sometimes, especially when he goes around saying he's the way'. For its part, the track 'Jesus in a Camper Van' contains this sentence: 'Even the son of God gets it hard sometimes, especially when he goes around, saying I am the way'. In his defence, Robbie said he heard the sentence from a young man who was in rehab with him. He said he found out it was from someone else's song only after recording it.

In 2002, Ludlow Music, owner of the rights to both versions of the song, won the case; Robbie was ordered to return 25 per cent of the track's royalties to the publisher. As a result, EMI Music decided to reissue the album; the song 'Jesus in a Camper Van' was replaced by a more recent track, 'It's Only Us'.

Just the title of the song, 'Jesus in a Camper Van', will have made more than one smile! Once again, we can sense Robbie's humour here, especially in the following sentence: 'I suppose even the son of God/Gets it hard sometimes'. It is not the most memorable track on the album, but it does make people smile at least.

'It's Only Us'

Writers: Robbie Williams, Guy Chambers
Duration: 2:50

This track was not present on the original edition of the album released in 1998. Originally, it was the song 'Jesus in a Camper Van' which occupied the seventh position in the album's track list.

Musically, 'It's Only Us' is the worthy heir to 'Let Me Entertain You' and 'Millennium'—an energetic, festive track that will satisfy more than one fan. Here we find a theme dear to Robbie at the time: that of the teenager who refuses to grow up and who prefers to devote his time to the pleasures of life. There is no ambiguity in the lyrics: 'And they want us to grow up/We don't want to get a job/We all need a decent rock/Where it's all kicking off'. Do you feel like dancing while listening to the track? This is quite the expected result!

It was originally released on the B-side of the single 'She's the One' in November 1999. Robbie even made a video for it. In fact, the song was used to promote the release of the *FIFA 2000* video game. In the video, Robbie is also shown as a CGI monkey. His virtual avatar embodies several characters in turn: that of the singer of Kiss from the music video 'Let Me Entertain You', the football player—in short, all the characters that Robbie had already played between 1997 and 1999. We regret probably only one thing in this track: its duration. It only lasts 2:52 and we would have liked a longer version!

'Heaven from Here'

Writers: Robbie Williams, Guy Chambers
Duration: 3:05

'Karma Killer'

Writers: Robbie Williams, Guy Chambers
Duration: 4:28

The song begins with very threatening whispers: 'You've been naughty … very very naughty'. Then comes a guitar riff, which Robbie leans on to deliver a series of reproaches to his interlocutor, and the words spoken are particularly harsh: 'Why haven't you managed to die yet'.

After a calm intro, the song transforms into something much more aggressive, bringing in a multitude of instruments—guitar, percussion, violins—whose repeated sounds hit the listener with persistence. The structure of the song is based on questioning, repetition, and emphasis. The track ends with barking, as if the singer had launched a pack of dogs towards his enemy.

This track is without a doubt the most violent of the album, and it contains the virility of the single 'Let Me Entertain You'.

'She's the One'

Writers:	Karl Wallinger
Duration:	4:18
Single release date:	8 November 1999
Charts:	No. 1 in UK

We tend to forget it or ignore it, but 'She's the One' is not a track written by Robbie—it is a cover! The track was composed by Karl Wallinger, from the band World Party. The song won an Ivor Novello Award in 1997; it even appeared in the soundtracks of two films in 1997 and 1998. But the amazing thing is the way Robbie's version of 'She's the One' was recorded. At the time, Guy Chambers and Steve Power simply called on the percussionist and guitarist of World Party to record the song! Although the two musicians never participated in the recording of the studio version created by World Party, this anecdote is still funny. When the single 'She's the One' was subsequently released, Robbie always claimed to be the author of that track, and never said it was a cover. Enraged, Wallinger ended up contacting Guy Chambers to ask him to insult Robbie.

Musically, there is an introduction on the piano, a method already used by Robbie on the very effective 'Angels'. 'She's the One' is surely the best-known love song in the singer's catalogue. The lyrics idealise the loved one, and just by reading them, we understand why the track became a No. 1: 'I was her/She was me/We were one/We were free/And if there's somebody calling me on/She's the one'. Quickly, over the tours, the song became one of the key moments of the concert, so much so that, on several occasions, Robbie took advantage of this song to allow several fans to propose to their partners during the concert!

The song takes off when Robbie speeds up and sings: 'When you said what you want to say/And you know the way you want to play it/You'll be so high you'll be flying'. The repetition of this verse, 'If there's somebody calling me on/She's the one', is particularly effective in building emotion in concert.

As for the music video, it is particularly successful and well in keeping with the theme of the song. Robbie plays a sports coach, helping a couple with figure skating. During a rehearsal, the male member of the pair ends up injuring himself and Robbie decides to replace him at short notice on competition day. It should be noted, moreover, that during rehearsals, Robbie is dressed all in black, exactly as in the 'Angels' video which brought him so much luck. The video then jumps to competition day, and Robbie ends up being a hit, stealing the show from the unlucky skater he replaced. The latter is being ridiculed, and his only consolation is to appear on crutches alongside Robbie and his partner when the couple's performance flowers are handed out. True to himself, the singer gives us several arrogant grimaces, characteristic of his 'bad boy' attitude of the time.

Extrapolating, you could almost tell yourself that the unlucky skater represents Karl Wallinger, from whom Robbie borrowed the song and stole the show!

'Man Machine'

Writers: Robbie Williams, Guy Chambers
Duration: 3:35

The track's vibe is similar to rock tracks from the album, like 'Karma Killer' or 'Phoenix from the Flames'. It is not the most impactful song on the album. We appreciate the badass style, which can be found in several tracks of the singer's first two albums. It is also a song that is especially appreciated in concert. However, it would be very adventurous to attempt to interpret the lyrics!

'These Dreams'

Writers: Robbie Williams, Guy Chambers
Duration: 5:08

'Stand Your Ground'

Writers: Robbie Williams, Guy Chambers
Duration: 3:28

'Stalker's Day Off (I've Been Hanging Around)'

Writers: Robbie Williams, Fil Eisler
Duration: 3:43

B-Sides linked to *I've Been Expecting You*

Love Cheat

Writers: Robbie Williams, Guy Chambers
Duration: 3:46
B-side of the single 'Millennium'

Although the lyrics of this track seem quite explicit at first glance, it is still difficult to understand what the song is about exactly. This is probably why it ended up on a B-side.

'Rome Munich Rome'

Writers: Robbie Williams, Guy Chambers
Duration: 3:05
B-side of the single 'Millennium'

It is hard to know why Robbie is talking about these two cities, Rome and Munich, here. *A priori*, the singer has no particular link with these two cities. We can probably imagine that he chose them solely for the musicality that their names give off. Apart from that, another very nice song, with a style similar to the songs from the album *I've Been Expecting You*.

'Antmusic'

Writers: Adam Ant, Marco Pirroni
Duration: 3:31
B-side of the single 'No Regrets'

This is a cover of the English band Adam and The Ants. The original version of the song was a hit in 1981, reaching No. 2 on the UK Singles Chart at the time.

'Deceiving Is Believing'

Writers: Robbie Williams, Guy Chambers
Duration: 4:30
B-side of the single 'No Regrets'

This song offers a nice alternative of calm verses and more rock choruses, as well as a good structure. Only the weak lyrics tend to disappoint the listener here.

'There She Goes (Live)'

Writers: Lee Mavers
Duration: 2:58
B-side of the single 'No Regrets'

'There She Goes' is one of Robbie's rare live tracks to exist in CD/streaming format. This is a cover of the British band The La's, whose original version was released in 1988; it was also their main hit. Why did Robbie cover this track? Probably because one of The La's drummers, Chris Sharrock, later became one of Robbie's band members!

'Happy Song'

Writers: Robbie Williams, Guy Chambers
Duration: 2:53
B-side of the single 'Strong'

After a very short Daft Punk intro, with a metallic voice saying 'Happy Song', the song switches to a traditionally pop rock track. We easily recognise the style of the album *I've Been Expecting You*, and this song could easily have found its place on the opus.

'Coke and Tears'

Writers: Robbie Williams, Guy Chambers
Duration: 4:24
B-side of the single 'She's the One/It's Only Us'

Unquestionably, one of Robbie's best B-sides! Again, the singer starts the song with an original intro. While in some songs Robbie starts with an extract from a fictional interview ('Teenage Millionaire', 'The Brits 2013'), here the song starts with a speaker, asking the public to sit down, because Robbie Williams is about to get on scene.

Robbie sings here in a rather soft voice, accompanied by military-style percussion, and a choir that grows in power throughout the song, tirelessly repeating 'Glory Glory Hallelujah'. The announcer intervenes again at the end of the song to conclude the fictitious concert, and he underlines ironically: 'Robbie Williams has left the building ... Oh no, I'm afraid he's come back for his coke'. The male choirs then repeat 'Glory Glory Hallelujah' again until the end of the song.

4

Sing When You're Winning

Release Date:	28 August 2000
Writers:	Robbie Williams, Guy Chambers, Kelvin Andrews, Nelson Pigford, Ekundayo Paris, Freddie Perren, Dino Fekaris
Producers:	Guy Chambers, Steve Power
Studios:	Master Rock Studios, Sarm Hook End
Recordings:	1999–2000
Duration:	75:58
Label:	Chrysalis/EMI

After the albums *Life thru a Lens* and *I've Been Expecting You*, which are at the origin of a huge hit ('Angels') and two No. 1 singles ('Millennium' and 'She's the One'), Robbie understood that he had set the bar very high and that it would be difficult to do better or even reach the same level. And yet, with *Sing When You're Winning*, the singer achieves a *tour de force*: a third album that builds on the successes of the first two, as well as achieving two other singles at the head of the UK Singles Chart, namely 'Rock DJ' and 'Eternity' (which was not released on the original 2000 edition, but on the summer 2001 collector's edition). While the artwork for *Life thru a Lens* was celebrity themed and the artwork for *I've Been Expecting You* was focused on James Bond, this time Robbie decided to devote himself to football for *Sing When You're Winning*. For this new opus, the singer teams up again with Guy Chambers and Steve Power, producers of the first two albums. This third album also features Kylie Minogue, marking the beginning of her big comeback.

'Let Love Be Your Energy'

Writers:	Robbie Williams, Guy Chambers
Duration:	4:59
Single release date:	9 April 2001
Charts:	No. 10 in UK

When I first discovered the *Sing When You're Winning* album, I was a little confused by the style of the album. After the first two albums, which were more British pop, Robbie takes a much more rock direction here, and you can hear it from the first track, 'Let Love Be Your Energy'. The track kicks off with the help of determined percussion, and immediately we discover that Robbie's voice has also matured. More frank, his voice carries the song like a Ferrari which would be all the rage on a highway. Physically, the singer has also changed: some tattoos have appeared, and his hair is longer.

All of this comes with a visual change as well. For the first time, a cartoon will serve as the music video for this track—the fourth single from the album.

Musically and lyrically, 'Let Love Be Your Energy' is a logical choice to open the album: positive lyrics, rock song—what an exciting choice! We feel a certain saturation when listening to the track. The track has a solid percussion, deafening guitar, singing and speaking, varying intonations, backing vocals, and children's voices. The show has started, no doubt about it.

'Better Man'

Writers:	Robbie Williams, Guy Chambers
Duration:	3:22
Single release date:	22 October 2001
Charts:	No. 4 in New Zealand

After the exuberant 'Let Love Be Your Energy', 'Better Man', a terribly effective ballad written in France, is a radical change. From the first seconds, we can only fall for this song, and even today, it is incomprehensible that this song was not released as a single in Europe! After a magnificent intro on the guitar, the singer's voice intervenes to deploy lyrics that border on perfection.

While 'Angels' sounded like a prayer, the first verse of 'Better Man' follows in the same vein. The singer first asks God to 'Send someone to love me/I need to rest in arms/Keep me safe from harm/In pouring rain', before then making promises in return: 'Lord, I'm doing all I can/To be a better man'. In the third verse, he asks for forgiveness: 'Go easy on my conscience/'Cause it's not my fault/I know I've been taught/To take the blame'. He took the opportunity to wink at the hit that brought him so much luck: 'Rest assured my angels'. The hearts of fans capsize when the bridge arrives, accompanied by touching violins and the heart-warming lyrics: 'Love is all around/Love is all around'.

Unfortunately, this track was only released as a single in some countries—Australia, New Zealand, and Latin America—and it was necessary to settle for a simple live performance as a music video. The song is also available in a Spanish version, under the title 'Ser Mejor'. This version was incorporated into the Latin American editions of the album.

'Rock DJ'

Writers:	Robbie Williams, Guy Chambers
Duration:	4:15
Single release date:	31 July 2000
Charts:	No. 1 in UK

Warning! Huge hit! When Robbie released his single 'Rock DJ' in the middle of the summer of 2000, he hit it big. Fans were certainly not ready to face such a monument. The singer achieves a double feat here: releasing both a single that would be a real hit and a music video that would remain one of the best in music video history. Who would have thought that Robbie would one day release a music video containing scenes of cannibalism?

But before we talk about the video, let us talk about the song. Not many people know that Robbie was inspired by singer Ian Dury (who died in March 2000) to write 'Rock DJ'. In fact, the two had met some time before as part of a charity trip for UNICEF. The song contains two samples: the first is from the track 'It's Ecstasy When You Lay Down Next to Me' by Barry White and the second is 'Can I Kick It' by the band A Tribe Called Quest.

'Rock DJ' also marks a turning point as it is the singer's first dance track. He calls on the characteristic features of dance songs from the '90s by repeating several times: 'It's time to move your body'. Ironically, Madonna would release an equally dance-genre and triumphant single, 'Music', at the same time. As Robbie sings: 'Singin' in the classes/Music for your masses'. Madonna cries out: 'Music makes the people come together/Music makes the bourgeoisie and the rebel'. In fact, both singles became No. 1 in sales only a few weeks apart. Aside from the dance theme, we also notice the sulphurous lyrics that Robbie does not hesitate to throw: 'I've got the gift/Gonna stick it in the goal' and 'Give no head/No backstage passes'. The track ends with a guitar riff that emphasises the excessive and bloody aspect of the images.

In the video, the singer dances dressed in a white top showing his most recent tattoos, like a Bruce Willis-type who came to save the world, surrounded by Top Models (the fashion of Top Models at the time still has some nice remnants). Desperate to attract attention, and taken by the excitement, he ends up removing all his clothes (including underpants decorated with a lion's head—which will become a symbol later), and goes so far as to tear off his own flesh to throw it in pasture to the young women who revolve around him. As for the DJ, he is embodied by another Top Model, the sublime Lauren Gold. If the efficiency of the music almost manages to make you forget the gore aspect of the scene, it was not the same for the television channels, which had to censor the video: some decided to broadcast it after midnight, while others preferred to broadcast another, totally different version. Indeed, the record company felt obligated to provide the media with an alternative version, where the singer is found in the studio.

But regardless of the censorship, the music video made so much noise that it was a hit for Robbie. Everyone talked about it, with the music video becoming a cult hit for its content, and EMI Music then decided to release the video on DVD and VHS (yes, there were still some in 2000). As for the charts, it was a hit, ranking No. 1 in sales.

'Supreme'

Writers: Robbie Williams, Guy Chambers, Dino Fekaris, Freddie Perren
Duration: 4:15
Single release date: 11 December 2000
Charts: No. 4 in UK

By the time 'Supreme' was released, many people were already aware of Guy Chambers and Robbie's ability to intelligently use well-known samples and incorporate them into effective pop songs. 'Supreme' is arguably the best example. To write and produce this song, Guy Chambers used two samples. The first comes from the French detective film, *Dernier Domicile Connu*, dating from 1970, and whose music is composed by François de Roubaix. It is with this sample, re-orchestrated, that the track begins. The second is easier to recognise from the first listen; it is a sample of the track 'I Will Survive' by Gloria Gaynor. This sample occurs in the musical bridge present in the middle of the piece. Its use is very easy to explain: when Robbie was recording his third album at the end of 1999, he heard the song while he was celebrating the transition to the year 2000 in Switzerland, and then he decided to sample it for use in one of his future songs. But we also know that Gloria's song had been a huge success in France the year before, as the official anthem of the World Cup, which France also won at home. The opportunity was too good. They incorporated a recent success skilfully into a new song, in order to appeal to the recent subconscious of the French public.

From then on, the magic and talent of Guy Chambers came together to give birth to another great Robbie hit: 'Supreme'. Moreover, the two men pushed opportunism to the maximum; not content to use a sample particularly known in France at that time, Robbie decided to record a French version of the track, and this single was even released in France before being released in the United Kingdom—a first in the career of the king of entertainment.

As if that was not enough, Robbie took another step towards excellence by writing words with Guy that were incredibly heart-warming (for the English version) and optimistic (for the French version). After a languid introduction, the song takes off in a melancholy manner, supported by powerful violins: 'When there's no love in town/This new century keeps bringing you down'. Helped by the disco anthem 'I Will Survive', the optimism is felt on the contrary in the French version of the song: 'Give the best of yourself/And you will find the supreme love/ Supreme love'. It should also be noted that even the original version in English contains French: female choirs indeed repeat: '*Aimer encore*'.

Another interesting aspect: 'Supreme', which is more of a work of art than a simple song because it is so full of detail, contains a few lines of rap, an element that Robbie loved to distil cleverly in several compositions at this time.

Finally, we note the excellent quality of the video, containing a multitude of details, as well as a self-mockery so characteristic of the singer. This time, he plays the role of Bob Williams, a fictional Formula 1 driver from the 1970s. In fact, it is a tribute to the driver Jackie Stewart. Some images of Stewart are included in the video.

'Kids'

Writers: Robbie Williams, Guy Chambers
Duration: 4:47
Single release date: 9 October 2000
Charts: No. 2 in UK

After four incredibly major tracks in the singer's career, Robbie does not give us a break. It follows with the song 'Kids', the famous duet with Kylie Minogue. The beautiful Australian is making her comeback at the end of the year 2000, and she has agreed with the king of Britpop to synchronise the release of the single, which is present on both *Sing When You're Winning*, and on Kylie's album, *Light Years*. But the single is considered to be Robbie's, as the artwork is in effect using his album's font.

Originally, it was Kylie who approached the English singer to ask him to write songs for his album *Light Years*, with the help of Guy Chambers. From this fruitful collaboration, three tracks were created: 'Loveboat', 'The Disco Needs You', and 'Kids'. Guy Chambers was also involved in writing a fourth track, 'I'm So High'.

This duet is a modern-day romance, between a tongue-in-cheek man and a sexy woman that many men would love to dance with. The song's theme is about impertinence and, of course, seduction.

We quickly recognise the style of the album *Sing When You're Winning*: a predominantly rock atmosphere, glamorous choirs, with strong percussion and guitar. Once again, Robbie dabbles in rap, with lyrics that left fans speechless: 'Press be asking do/I care for sodomy/I don't know, yeah, probably'. This has been Robbie's trademark since the start of his solo career: bold, raw lyrics that testify to the singer's excesses. He refuses nothing, and his various provocations are not even condemned by the media.

On the music video front, we are dealing with a rather sober atmosphere: the couple, all dressed in black, are surrounded by dancers in black underwear. There is a choreography and style here that is widely used in Kylie's music videos, but it is also a reference to the choreography from the movie *Grease*. Despite the apparent sobriety, the video ends all the same on a scorching scene: the singer takes off her clothes to join her partner in a swimming pool, and the opening of the bottle of Champagne at the very end of the video will have made them smile more than once!

'If It's Hurting You'

Writers: Robbie Williams, Guy Chambers
Duration: 4:10

'Singing for the Lonely'

Writers: Robbie Williams, Guy Chambers
Duration: 4:31

'Love Calling Earth'

Writers: Robbie Williams, Guy Chambers, Kelvin Andrews
Duration: 4:05

'Knutsford City Limits'

Writers: Robbie Williams, Guy Chambers, Kelvin Andrews
Duration: 4:45

'Forever Texas'

Writers: Robbie Williams, Guy Chambers
Duration: 3:37

'Forever Texas' is undoubtedly the song which gives us (surely without Robbie knowing it at the time) a glimpse of what will be his next pop rock album, *Escapology*. Strongly anchored in rock, backing vocals, and American vibes, the track appeals to lovers of Texas. This is what is most astonishing with *Sing When You're Winning*: although the singer still lived in the United Kingdom at the time, many songs seem straight out of the Wild West! It is rarely sung in concert, yet that is what this warm song is intended for.

'By All Means Necessary'

Writers: Robbie Williams, Guy Chambers
Duration: 4:45

'The Road to Mandalay'

Writers: Robbie Williams, Guy Chambers
Duration: 3:57
Single release date: 9 July 2001

The album ends with a new ballad, which has been released as a single—or rather as a double single. While on the previous album, the double single 'She's the One/It's Only Us' had been a hit, EMI Music decided to try it again, this time with 'Eternity/The Road to Mandalay'. The bet paid off, as 'Eternity' was also No. 1 in sales, as was 'She's the One'.

Again accompanied by an omnipresent guitar, Robbie unrolls here a superb song which did not fail to crack the young women, as he knows so well how to do. But behind the paradisiacal aspect of the song—'What a lovely holiday, there's nothing funny left to say'—there is in fact a certain darkness that never leaves the singer:

'Everything I touched was golden/Everything I loved got broken'. The subtlety of the lyrics lies in the very fine line that separates heaven from hell. Despite soft and peaceful music, the singer slips a few disturbing words: 'Look down the barrel of a gun and feel the moon replace the sun'.

It is this discretion that is also found in the music video. For the first time, Robbie is shooting a double video, consisting of the tracks 'The Road to Mandalay' and 'Eternity'. The two videos together form a fourteen-minute film, entitled *Rob by Nature*, which was filmed in the south of France. In the first part, 'The Road to Mandalay', we let ourselves be drawn into a blissful setting, where recklessness reigns. But without warning, we switch to a mini-film featuring a gang of thugs including Robbie. Accompanied by his fellow criminals, Robbie participates in a robbery: money, sun, pretty girls, and dreamy scenery are waiting for you.

'Eternity'

Writers:	Robbie Williams, Guy Chambers
Duration:	5:00
Single release date:	9 July 2001
Charts:	No. 1 in UK

'The Road to Mandalay' music video follows on to the second track, 'Eternity', which is arguably one of Robbie's best ballads, alongside 'Angels' and 'Better Man'. The video alternates between footage of the robbery and particularly romantic scenes where the singer is accompanied by a pretty blonde bride. It ends with the tragic arrest of the malefactor singer by the police.

In terms of words, we can hardly dream of better: 'You were there for summer dreaming/And you gave me what I need/And I hope you find your freedom/For eternity'. Listening to these words, we can only melt: 'We sat and watched the sun go down/Picked a star before we lost the moon'.

Just like 'Angels' and 'She's the One', it is at the piano that Robbie calls on us to deliver that wonderful melody that is 'Eternity'. Released at the very beginning of summer, and accompanied by a magnificent video, the track was directly ranked No. 1 in sales when it was released, making this Robbie's fourth No.1 single in less than three years.

It should also be noted that the song involves a distinguished guest: Brian May of Queen. Brian is the guitarist who accompanies Robbie on this track. The reason for his presence is simple: at the time, the two men recorded together the cover of 'We Are the Champions', from the movie *A Knight's Tale*. Moreover, as these various collaborations arose, rumours of the reformation of the band Queen with Robbie as leader were heard. But it was Adam Lambert who ultimately won the game many years later.

B-Sides linked to *Sing When You're Winning*

'Dance With the Devil'

Writers: Robbie Williams, Guy Chambers, Kelvin Andrews Mould, Daniel Spencer Mould
Duration: 2:51
Song extract from the *Where Egos Dare* DVD

This song was only released on the *Where Egos Dare* DVD. This is not a single, but rather a bonus track, much to the delight of fans, especially since, for this song, Robbie shot a music video where he appears shirtless, in the middle of his band.

'Talk to Me'

Writers: Robbie Williams, Fil Eisler
Duration: 3:28
B-side of the single 'Rock DJ'

One of the few songs composed with the help of Fil Eisler, guitarist of the band during the first few years of Robbie's solo career. The song is rather calm, but with some rock impulses all the same.

'Karaoke Star'

Writers: Robbie Williams, Guy Chambers
Duration: 4:10
B-side of the single 'Kids'

'Kill Me or Cure Me'

Writers: Robbie Williams, Guy Chambers
Duration: 2:14
B-side of the single 'Kids'

'John's Gay'

Writers: Robbie Williams, Guy Chambers
Duration: 3:40
B-side of the single 'Kids'

'Often'

Writers: Gary Nuttall
Duration: 2:46
B-side of the single 'Kids'

'Don't Do Love'

Writers: Robbie Williams, Guy Chambers
Duration: 4:56
B-side of the single 'Supreme'

As so often, Robbie alternates between very calm verses and much more energetic verses—an infallible method when you want to seduce the public and attract its attention. While in 1999, he sang 'She's the One', he says here 'I'm not the one'. We quickly let ourselves be convinced by this song with its rather effective melody.

'Come Take Me Over'

Writers: Robbie Williams, Guy Chambers
Duration: 4:13
B-side of the single 'Supreme'

'My Way (Live At Manchester Arena)'

Writers: Gilles Thibaut, Jacques Revaux
Duration: 4:32
B-side of the single 'Let Love Be Your Energy'

In October 2000, Robbie performed the famous song 'My Way' in Manchester. It is this version which is teased on the single of 'Let Love Be Your Energy'. Over the years, Robbie has performed this song many times. Among the notable performances, there is obviously the one performed on 10 October 2001 at the Royal Albert Hall, for the promotion of the album *Swing When You're Winning*. By force of circumstance, Robbie's cover has become a classic, and one of the favourite songs of fans when the singer performs it at the end of the concert.

'Rolling Stone'

Writers: Robbie Williams, Guy Chambers
Duration: 3:30
B-side of the single 'Let Love Be Your Energy'

Here is a particularly successful B-side. Catchy and dynamic, this track wakes you up. It fits purely and simply in the spirit of the album *Sing When You're Winning*. It can be identified as a very good Britpop track, with a clear influence from the Beatles.

'Toxic'

Writers: Robbie Williams, Guy Chambers
Duration: 3:48
B-side of the single 'Eternity/The Road to Mandalay'

A fan favourite! After an intro that suggests wind, cold, and loneliness, the singer immerses us in a dark and depressing atmosphere that leads us to drama: 'Oh I wanna cry but I don't make a sound'.

'Disco Delilah'

Writers: Robbie Williams, Guy Chambers
Duration: 1:06

This is not a B-side. It was recorded in 2000, but Robbie leaked it in 2013.

5

Swing When You're Winning

Release date:	19 November 2001
Writers:	Robbie Williams, Guy Chambers, Al Jolson, Bertolt Brecht, Billy Rose, Bob Russell, Bobby Darin, Carson Parks, Charles Trenet, Cole Porter, Dave Dreyer, Duke Ellington, Ervin Drake, George Gershwin, Harold Arlen, Ira Gershwin, Irving Mills, Jack Lawrence, Jerry Jeff Walker, Jimmy Van Heusen, Johnny Mercer, Kurt Weill, Lorenz Hart, Marc Blitzstein, Nat King Cole, Richard Rodgers, Sammy Cahn
Producers:	Guy Chambers, Steve Power
Studios:	Capitol Studios, Sony Music Studios, Air Lyndhurst Recording Studios, Angel Recording Studios, Electric Lady Studios, Battery Studios
Recordings:	2001
Duration:	53:00
Label:	Chrysalis/EMI

Robbie Williams is primarily known for two aspects: his emergence in a boy band in the early '90s and his Britpop career as a solo singer. The general audience is less familiar with his crooning skills, despite his famous duet with Nicole Kidman. Yet from 2001, the singer would work in the swing genre more, both on 'side projects' (featurings, soundtracks of films, etc.) and on albums entirely dedicated to the swing style (*Swing When You're Winning*, *Swings Both Ways*, and, to a lesser extent, *The Christmas Present*). Ironically enough, his swing albums often sell far more than his pop albums; in other words, you could almost say that Robbie is more successful as a swing singer!

When Robbie entered the studio in August 2001 to record *Swing When You're Winning*, his first swing album, he took no risks: he locked himself in the legendary Capitol Studios in Hollywood, surrounded by a classic orchestra. Why this choice? Quite simply because Frank Sinatra was the first artist to record an album there, and the crooner returned there regularly until the end of the 1950s. Always in order to play it safe, Robbie chose to record only covers for this album, with the exception of the first song: 'I Will Talk and Hollywood Will Listen'. The album was released under the Capitol label, and even the singer's style of dress on the album's cover and booklet strived to mimic Frank Sinatra's look.

'I Will Talk and Hollywood Will Listen'

Writers: Robbie Williams, Guy Chambers
Duration: 3:08
Single release date: 26 August 2002

'I Will Talk and Hollywood Will Listen' is the only original track featured on the *Swing When You're Winning* album, and it is also the album's opening song. After two successful double singles ('She's the One/It's Only Us' in 1999 and 'Eternity/The Road to Mandalay' in 2001), EMI Music tried to renew the winning duo with a new double single in the spring of 2002: 'Mr Bojangles/I Will Talk and Hollywood Will Listen'. However, this time the magic did not work. There could be several reasons for this. First, this single came out in the spring in Germany and in August in Australia, a less favourable season for swing tracks, which are more optimised for the holiday season. Then, no new music video was made for the occasion: the video of 'Mr Bojangles' is only a live extract of the concert at the Royal Albert Hall, given six months earlier, and no video was made for 'I Will Talk and Hollywood Will Listen'. Peculiarly, in Germany, 'Mr Bojangles' is listed first (moreover, the single in Europe was released only in Germany), while in Australia, 'I Will Talk and Hollywood Will Listen' is listed first on the cover art.

Composed by Robbie and Guy Chambers, it sounds great, and its style and elegance are so remarkable that you might think this is a Frank Sinatra cover, but it is not!

One of the hallmarks of Robbie's style is clearly recognised in the lyrics: the emphasis on an oversized ego. We can only smile when reading the lyrics: 'Kevin Spacey would call on the phone/But I'd be too busy'. His interpretation of the song during the concert on 10 October 2001 at the Royal Albert Hall is particularly successful. With elegance and a smile, he manages to take the crowd with him: prompted by brilliant words and solemn music, the audience rejoices at the slightest provocation, especially when he exclaims: 'Mr. Spielberg look just what you're missing!!'

Even today, the sight of this performance gives me chills and sometimes puts tears in my eyes. This interpretation surprises us with the feat it puts in place: the singer manages, through his arrogance and his ego, to strangely arouse emotion and respect.

'Mack the Knife'

Writers: Bertold Brecht, Kurt Weill, Marc Blitzstein
Duration: 3:24

'Somethin' Stupid'

Writers: Clarence Carson Parks II
Duration: 2:50
Single release date: 10 December 2001
Charts: No. 1 in UK

The duet between Robbie and Australian actress Nicole Kidman was one of the major musical events of 2001. In recording this single, the singer had arguably one of the greatest hits of his career. Not only did he manage to afford the talents of one of the most beautiful actresses of the moment, but in addition, his single was a true triumph. Ranked directly at No. 1 in sales upon its release, the song saw Robbie land his fifth No. 1 single in just five years, with over 1 million copies sold to date. 'Somethin' Stupid' is indeed the singer's third best-selling single: 'Angels' ranks first, with an incredible 2,287,000 copies, followed by 'Rock DJ' which has no less than 1,427,500 copies sold. 'Somethin' Stupid' therefore climbed to third place with 1,005,000 copies sold to date.

The success of this duet can be explained by the quality of the music video. Fans will be delighted to see Robbie and Nicole reunite on screen for one song, plus the music video wows audiences for its magical, funny, festive, and sexy vibe. In the video, Robbie and Nicole take on the role of a young couple experiencing perfect love in a very retro setting over the holiday season. The singer cannot resist the temptation to slip us a few grimaces as he knows how to do them so well (you know, his talent for playing the little duck), and the video gradually goes from the sweet *bon-enfant* serenade to a sexier atmosphere.

The two artists unfortunately never performed the track together on stage. While promoting the single in December 2001, Robbie found himself performing the track solo; Nicole was only present virtually, playing the music video in the background during the performance.

'Do Nothing Till You Hear From Me'

Writers: Duke Ellington, Bob Russell
Duration: 2:58

'It Was a Very Good Year'

Writers: Ervin Drake
Duration: 4:28

'Straighten Up and Fly Right'

Writers: Nat King Cole, Irving Mills
Duration: 2:36

'Well, Did You Evah'

Writers: Cole Porter
Duration: 3:50

'Mr Bojangles'

Writers: Jerry Jeff Walker
Duration: 3:18
Single release date: 10 March 2002

Released as a single in the spring of 2002, accompanied by 'I Will Talk and Hollywood Will Listen', 'Mr Bojangles' is another highlight of the album. The best way to appreciate this song is to watch the live performance that the singer gave at the Royal Albert Hall on 10 October 2001. Robbie starts the song by whistling before moving on to the lyrics. His interpretation is stunning; just watch his look, his smile, and his grimaces to fully appreciate his incredible emotion. Every time I watch this video, tears take over! It is hard to ignore Robbie's crooning skills here. This performance, like the whole of this unique concert, testifies to his immense talent.

'One for My Baby'

Writers: Johnny Mercer, Harold Arlen
Duration: 4:18

'Things'

Writers: Bobby Darin
Duration: 3:22

'Ain't That a Kick in the Head'

Writers: Jimmy Van Heusen, Sammy Cahn
Duration: 2:28

'They Can't Take That Away from Me'

Writers: George Gershwin, Ira Gershwin
Duration: 3:07

'Have You Met Miss Jones?'

Writers: Lorenz Hart, Richard Rogers
Duration: 2:34

'Me and My Shadow'

Writers: Dave Dreyer, Al Jolson, Billy Rose
Duration: 3:16

'Beyond the Sea'

Writers: Charles Trenet, Lawrence
Duration: 4:27
Taken from the *Finding Nemo* movie soundtrack.

The album *Swing When You're Winning* has the merit of containing two tracks that have been used in two film soundtracks: 'Have You Met Miss Jones?' for *Bridget Jones's Diary* and 'Beyond the Sea' for the computer-animated adventure film *Finding Nemo*.

This song is the English adaptation of the song 'La Mer' by Charles Trenet. The sea-themed track, as well as the song's swing style, was perfect for musically illustrating the story of the fish named Nemo.

The song gives pride of place to instruments, elegance, and lightness, and we can say that Robbie's interpretation here is impeccable. The song was the subject of a performance at the Royal Albert Hall, during the singer's unique concert on 10 October 2001. 'Beyond the Sea' was never released as a single at the time, but oddly, a few years later, its introduction on streaming platforms benefited from an original cover, using the artwork of the album *Swing When You're Winning*.

'The Lady is a Tramp'

Writers: Richard Rogers, Lorenz Hart
Duration: 2:56

'That's Life'

Writers: Dean Kay, Kelly Gordon
Duration: 3:07

6

Escapology

Release date:	18 November 2002
Writers:	Robbie Williams, Guy Chambers, Adrian Deevoy, Boots Ottestad, Ashley Hamilton, Daniel Pierre
Producers:	Guy Chambers, Steve Power
Studios:	Tower of Power Studios, Mayfair Recording Studios, Air Lyndhurst Recording Studios, O'Henry Sound Studios, Conway Studios, Capitol Studios, Angel Recording Studios
Recordings:	2001–2002
Duration:	73:55
Label:	Chrysalis/EMI

By the beginning of 2002, Robbie had released four albums in five years. His first deal as a solo singer ended with the album *Swing When You're Winning* in 2001, and understandably, all the majors wanted to sign with the King of Britpop. With four No. 1 bestselling albums and five UK No. 1 singles, the singer was worth gold.

The negotiations between Robbie and various record companies lasted several months. Finally, on 2 October 2002, the news broke: Robbie re-signed with EMI Music, for a hefty contract of £80 million—one of the most important deals in pop music history. We then learnt that the contract included four new albums as well as two greatest hits compilations. To negotiate the deal, the singer had a golden card in his game: a brand-new album, ready to be released, called *Escapology*. Written once again with the help of his mentor, Guy Chambers, EMI knew they had the potential to make the contract profitable, and this time, the label intended to promote the album around the world, including Japan and the USA, so that their investment paid off.

However, as nothing ever goes as planned, EMI Music first faced a crisis the day after the signing of the contract: Guy Chambers could not agree with Robbie on the terms of his new deal, and after several hours of negotiations, the two men put an end to their six years of collaboration. One can imagine the panic this news must have triggered in EMI headquarters. Fortunately, *Escapology* was a huge success: apart from being No. 1 in sales like his four previous albums, it was met with critical acclaim and the album would subsequently be considered the singer's best. Four singles were taken from the album: 'Feel', 'Come Undone', 'Something Beautiful', and 'Sexed Up'. Apart from 'Feel', which was unanimous, fans were later baffled by the other choices. Indeed, how do you choose 'Something Beautiful' and 'Sexed Up', for example, when other tracks, like 'Love Somebody', 'Revolution', and 'Handsome Man' are undoubtedly much more effective? However, despite the departure of Guy Chambers, and despite these weird choices, the success of the album was not affected, and the tour the following year was a huge success. The singer met sales records that would end up in the *Guinness Book of World Records* for the three concerts events given in Knebworth in August 2003.

'How Peculiar'

Writers: Robbie Williams, Guy Chambers
Duration: 3:13

'Feel'

Writers: Robbie Williams, Guy Chambers
Duration: 4:24
Single release date: 10 October 2002
Charts: No. 4 in UK

Of Robbie's five No. 1 singles, released between 1998 and 2001, three of them were ballads. It was not surprising then that the singer tried for his sixth with a new ballad, 'Feel', the first single from *Escapology*. However, the single only ranked fourth in the UK Singles Chart, though Robbie was still untouchable, and the media easily 'forgave' him for fourth place in the charts.

Although released in 2002, this song was written in 1999! We had to wait three years to discover this new track.

I still remember the day I heard 'Feel' for the first time. Robbie brings strong emotions that intensify throughout the song. Accompanied by an omnipresent piano, a mid-tempo rhythm, and a guitar that encourages dance, the singer here expresses his desire for love: 'I just wanna feel/Real love feel the home that I live in'. He also expresses a depressive thought: 'I don't wanna die/But I ain't keen on living either'. Vocally, we find here a slightly scratched voice, which ends up reaching heights of despair: 'And I need to feel/Real love and the love ever after'.

While in the first two albums, we had a Robbie with an almost-shaved hair, then a slightly longer cut for *Sing When You're Winning*, this new album is the occasion to sport a new cut. This time, he goes for even longer hair, including that famous crest that is the hallmark of the album.

For the music video, Robbie once again surrounds himself with a woman to stage this love song. It is Daryl Hannah who accompanies him in this video, which exists in two versions: a black and white version, broadcast on television, and a colour version, which appeared on the DVD single. Filming took place in Canada, while Daryl was shooting Quentin Tarantino's movie *Kill Bill*. The very American and country setting of the video fits perfectly with the album's cover, which was shot in Los Angeles.

Over the years, the track became one of the essential pillars of the singer's concerts, just like 'Rock DJ', 'Millennium', or 'Angels'.

'Something Beautiful'

Writers:	Robbie Williams, Guy Chambers
Duration:	4:48
Single release date:	28 July 2003
Charts:	No. 3 in UK

Listening to the track, we quickly discover that the style is very similar to that of Elton John. The resemblance, both vocal and rhythmic, is striking. However, Robbie and Guy Chambers originally planned to give this song to his friend Tom Jones, but Robbie finally decided to keep the song.

'Something Beautiful' is characterised by rather light, upbeat, and happy lyrics—unusual as this is not an atmosphere to which Robbie had accustomed us. But the point of this cheerfulness is that it encourages fans to sing along to the song, so much so does it convey joy at lightning speed; this is without a doubt the effect that was expected.

If the lyrics seem quite enigmatic at first listen, they take on their full meaning in the music video. It features reality TV candidates who try to win a singing competition, as in *The X Factor*. For the shoot, Robbie organised a real singing competition. Fans of the singer had to attend a casting to sing like their idol, and it is the cast and the fictional show he is from that are shown in the video. Of note is the presence of Robbie's father, Pete Conway, who has agreed to play the game and become one of the show's judges.

On the charts side, the single managed to climb to No. 3, one place better than the highly respected 'Feel'!

'Monsoon'

Writers:	Robbie Williams, Guy Chambers
Duration:	3:46

'Sexed Up'

Writers:	Robbie Williams, Guy Chambers
Duration:	4:19
Single release date:	3 November 2003
Charts:	No. 10 in UK

Here is a very strange fate for a song. Originally, 'Sexed Up' was released as a demo in 1998, on the B-side of 'No Regrets'. Four years later, Robbie decided to incorporate it into his album *Escapology* and to release it as a single. In fact, this song was written for Natalie Imbruglia, who rejected it.

After the darkness of 'Feel' and 'Come Undone', Robbie finds the same register here, with the lyrics of 'Sexed Up', in which he evokes a breakup: 'Why don't we break up?/There's nothing left to say'. The disappointment is such that he goes so far as to utter very harsh words: 'Screw you, I didn't like your taste, anyway'.

In fact, if you exclude 'Something Beautiful', the other three singles taken from *Escapology* are pretty dark—a rather new atmosphere in the theme of the singer, even if we had already been able to glimpse certain aspects on the previous albums. However, these three singles are not representative of the album: many songs like 'Love Somebody', 'Revolution', 'Handsome Man', or 'Hot Fudge' are much more optimistic.

'Love Somebody'

Writers: Robbie Williams, Guy Chambers
Duration: 4:10

One of the most beautiful tracks on the album. The song starts slowly on the piano, quickly joined by Robbie. It then ramps up quickly: first with the addition of percussion, strings, then backing vocals at the end.

The text begins with a certain poetry, built around metaphors about time, then followed by cries of despair—the despair of loving and being happy: 'Trying to love somebody/Just want to love somebody right now/There's just no pleasing me'. You have to recognise Robbie's writing skills in this song. The theme of time is used extensively throughout the song: 'And it's hope that springs eternal for everyone/ Got a lifetime in a second oh the damage done'. Much like in 'Angels', we find here the theme of prayer: oppressed by time, Robbie prays to God so that he can find love as soon as possible. It is regrettable that this song was never exploited on tour, where it would have found its place perfectly, for the power it gives off.

'Revolution'

Writers: Robbie Williams, Guy Chambers
Duration: 5:44

Another song that would have found its place in single or on tour. After the powerful 'Love Somebody', the song 'Revolution' is a song with a comforting and catchy melody, interpreted here in duet with the singer Rose Stone.

The meaning of the lyrics is, however, more mysterious than on the previous song. We feel more that Robbie wanted to play here with words and their poetry. Between dance and romance, 'Revolution' seduces us with its simplicity, naturalness, and beauty.

'Handsome Man'

Writers: Robbie Williams, Guy Chambers, Adrian Deevoy
Duration: 3:56

This is Robbie's end to a winning trio, comprised of 'Love Somebody', 'Revolution', and now 'Handsome Man'.

This song is amazing, and it is a fan favourite on this album—as much for his music as for his words. If there were to be a Robbie Williams-style flirting manual, this is definitely the song to remember. The lyrics are full of humour and winks. The singer does not hesitate to unwrap his oversized ego to seduce us: 'Hello. Did you miss me?/I know I'm hard to resist/[…]/It's hard to be humble/When you're so fucking big/Did you ever meet a sexier male chauvinist pig'. The stage is set! Further, the singer proudly affirms: 'I'm the one who put the Brits in celebrity'. Enough to tear us away from a smile! Musically, the song quickly accelerates in a whirlwind of happiness, where ego and euphoria happily coexist, aided by a guitar advancing with a determined step.

'Come Undone'

Writers: Robbie Williams, Ashley Hamilton, Per Kristian Ottestad, Daniel Pierre
Duration: 4:34
Single release date: 31 March 2003
Charts: No. 4 in UK

Here is the track of discord! Although Guy Chambers produced this track, he was not involved in the writing of it. In fact, Guy hates this song. He hates it so much that he would have indicated to Robbie that if the latter decided to put it on the tour, he would refuse to play it. In the meantime, Guy did not need to choose to make such a decision, the two men having separated a few months before the tour when the deal was signed with EMI.

I have to say that I must be one of the few fans that does not like this song. I never liked the style of the song, which to me sounds like a caricature of a rock track. However, we know that, usually, Robbie is not the type to give in to the cliché.

Other than 'Nan's Song', 'Come Undone' is the only track that Guy Chambers did not write on the album. It was written with Ashley Hamilton, the son-in-law of Rod Stewart. Strangely, at the time of recording the album, Robbie dated Rachel Hunter, Rod Stewart's ex-wife at the time!

'Come Undone' is not the only collaboration between the 'Angels' singer and Ashley. In 2001, Robbie introduced a new song, 'Wimmin', on tour. He subsequently gave this track to Ashley, who released it as a single, one on which Robbie provides the backing vocals.

With 'Come Undone', fans rediscovered the darkness that gives the singer so much charm. The song sounds like a long confession in which he admits all his sins.

Above all, you must dwell on the music video. You could almost imagine this one taking place the day after 'Let Me Entertain You'. In the video, Robbie wakes up in a cluttered Hollywood penthouse with many friends asleep all over the house. Over the course of the images, we see a series of sequences unfolding which testify to all the possible excesses of Californian life: alcohol, sex, drugs, etc. Filmed by the famous Jonas Akerlund, the music video caused scandal and censorship upon its release, both for the lyrics and for the images. Several versions of the video exist, including one where Robbie simulates sex acts with men. While MTV decided to censor the video, EMI reserved the uncensored version for the DVD single, which was released at the same time as the single. The song was banned by BBC Radio 2, refusing to play it because of its explicit content and references to drugs.

At the end of the day, 'Come Undone' represents the singer's most triumphant rock track. On tour, we have to admit that he brings crowds together and creates almost unanimity among both women and men.

'Me and My Monkey'

Writers: Robbie Williams, Guy Chambers
Duration: 7:12

At seven minutes and twelve seconds, 'Me and My Monkey' is the longest track on the album, and possibly the longest of Robbie's career. Ironically, the song was written five minutes before going on stage in Taiwan.

The song acts more as a story told by Robbie, against a backdrop of Mexican music, embodied by a trumpet. It quickly became a fan favourite, and for this reason, Robbie has performed it several times on tour.

With 'Me and My Monkey', Robbie takes us to a strange world, and the presence of this monkey somewhere symbolises the singer's quirk, whose life has often been torn between angel and demon.

This song was not released as a single, but an official music video was still made: a cartoon of plasticine characters depicts the adventures of Robbie and his friend the monkey.

This song had a particularly disturbing and tragic fate. On 1 October 2017, Stephen Paddock, an American, fired several thousand bullets from his hotel room in Las Vegas at the crowd gathered for a music festival. The tragedy left fifty-eight dead and 527 injured. The media very quickly made the connection between the drama and the song, because coincidences are noted. Indeed, in the song, Robbie and his monkey ('with a dream and a gun') go to the Mandalay Bay Hotel in Las Vegas, the same hotel where the shooter was located. But what is more disturbing still is that Robbie mentions the thirty-third floor of the hotel ('And at the elevator I hit the 33rd floor"'), whereas the shooter himself was just one floor below, on the thirty-second floor. Finally, Robbie also sings about the monkey: 'Hoping my monkey/ Don't point that gun at anyone'. If no connection was found between the author of the shots and Robbie's song, the astonishing coincidences between the drama and the lyrics have chilled more than one.

'Song 3'

Writers: Robbie Williams, Guy Chambers
Duration: 3:48

'Hot Fudge'

Writers: Robbie Williams, Guy Chambers
Duration: 4:08

The vibe of the *Escapology* album is clearly American. We had already had an American taste with the album *Sing When You're Winning*. With an album cover shot in Los Angeles, and an easily identifiable musical universe, *Escapology* is fully American-oriented and 'Hot Fudge' is arguably the most American song on the album.

From the start, the track takes us into a saloon atmosphere, with the thundering piano opening the way, followed by a very country 'Hii-Ah' blown by Robbie.

In a festive atmosphere, the singer invites us to Los Angeles throughout the song: 'Mother, things have got to change/I'm moving to LA'.

This song also gives pride of place to a rather long and pleasant musical bridge. 'Hot Fudge' plays its light and enjoyable song role very well. It is easy to get caught up in the game, and it is hard to resist the urge to sing and dance to this 'Hot Fudge'!

The song has never been released as a single, but a promo CD has been pressed, and the track was sung several times on tour, to the delight of fans.

'Cursed'

Writers: Robbie Williams, Guy Chambers, Adrian Deevoy
Duration: 4:01

'Nan's Song'

Writers: Robbie Williams
Duration: 3:50

This is the first song that Robbie wrote entirely on his own, without the help of Guy Chambers. It is dedicated to his grandmother, Bertha Talbot. Robbie also had the letter 'B' tattooed behind his ear, in reference to her.

'How Peculiar – Reprise (Hidden Track)'

Writers: Robbie Williams, Guy Chambers
Duration: 2:18

'I Tried Love (Hidden Track)'

Writers: Robbie Williams, Guy Chambers
Duration: 3:31

B-Sides Linked to *Escapology*

'Nobody Someday'

Writers: Robbie Williams, Guy Chambers
Duration: 2:53
B-side of the single 'Feel'

This song bears the same name as the documentary *Nobody Someday*, released on DVD in July 2002, a few months before the release of the single 'Feel'.

This is a ballad where Robbie sings very softly, accompanied simply by a guitar and the fictitious noise of crickets in the background.

'You're History'

Writers: Robbie Williams, Guy Chambers
Duration: 2:04
B-side of the single 'Feel'

A Western atmosphere dominates this song, supported by rock-style instrumentals and by lyrics that talk about guns, cigarettes, girls, guys, fights, and diamonds.

'One Fine Day'

Writers: Robbie Williams
Duration: 1:56
B-side of the single 'Come Undone'

'One Fine Day' is produced by Boots Ottestad, one of the composers of the single 'Come Undone', from which it is taken. Even if the meaning of the lyrics is quite obscure, we are quickly seduced by the melody and the chorus of this song.

'Happy Easter (War is Coming)'

Writers: Robbie Williams
Duration: 4:03
B-side of the single 'Come Undone'

'Happy Easter (War is Coming)' refers to a song by John Lennon, titled 'Happy Xmas (War is Over)'. John Lennon's song was released in December 1971 to protest the Vietnam War.

Almost thirty years later, Robbie took inspiration from John Lennon's song at the very moment when the United States was embarking on a new war: Iraq. While the war in Iraq indeed began on 20 March 2003, the song 'Happy Easter (War is Coming)' was released on 31 March as a B-side from the single 'Come Undone'—a rather risky decision when we know that, at the same time, Robbie was releasing the American edition of his album *Escapology*, hoping to finally be able to break into the land of Uncle Sam. The singer was also forced to deny the link between his song and the war in Iraq because it could be considered an unpatriotic movement. Madonna suffered the same criticism; when she decided to release her music video 'American Life' on 31 March (this one particularly explicit and going against George Bush's policy), she was forced to cancel the release of his video the following day.

Even though Robbie does not explicitly talk about the Iraq War, he still sings: 'Singing I won't go to war/Lay down my guns/What are we fighting for, for'. That said, it is possible that the controversy did not go beyond the borders of the United Kingdom. First, it is a B-side, but in addition, no video was made for this song, and finally the track was not released in the USA.

'Berliner Star'

Writers: Robbie Williams, Boots Ottestad
Duration: 3:52
B-side of the single 'Something Beautiful'

Escapology had a particular focus on rock, and especially in the style of the English bad boy. Just read this excerpt from the lyrics: '*Auf Wiedersehen* Berliner Star/You rock like a bastard, blaster'. This song was composed, once more, with the help of Boots Ottestad, one of the main collaborators of the *Escapology* album.

'Coffee, Tea & Sympathy'

Writers: Robbie Williams, Billy Morrison, Glen Ballard
Duration: 4:35
B-side of the single 'Something Beautiful'

When Robbie decided to spend more time in the United States in the early 2000s, he became close to several rock and even heavy metal figures, such as Brian May of the band Queen, Ozzy Osbourne, Marilyn Manson, and Billy Morrison. We had already seen Robbie and Billy together in 2001, notably in the 'We Are the Champions' music video. Here they are again reunited for the composition of this track, 'Coffee, Tea & Sympathy', to which the composer Glen Ballard came to help.

Ironically, the track is far from rock; it is more of a mid-tempo track, but enjoyable enough to be seduced again by Robbie's talents.

'Appliance of Science'

Writers: Robbie Williams, Max Beesley
Duration: 4:52
B-side of the single 'Sexed Up'

The presence of Max Beesley in the writing of this song is unsurprising as Max spent a lot of time with Robbie in 2003 and even participated in the 2003 tour. This track is highly provocative, with Robbie singing: 'Don't believe in Jesus Christ/

Since I believed in your cocaine'. We note the amusing passage of the song in which the singer imitates a TV host by stating a series of miscellaneous facts.

'Get a Little High'

Writers: Robbie Williams, Boots Ottestad
Duration: 3:56
B-side of the single 'Sexed Up'

Robbie sometimes tends to repeat himself! While in the title 'One Fine Day' (B-side of the 'Come Undone' single), he sang 'In the middle of the night/You'll wake up in it', in 'Get a Little High', he sings: 'You wake up in the middle of/The thunder of a scream'. When we know that the two songs ended up on the American edition of *Escapology*, we can say that the singer did not show much originality here!

But 'Get a Little High', composed again with the help of Boots Ottestad, is a rather comforting song, with very musical lyrics. A song that could very well have found its place in concert.

'Big Beef'

Writers: Robbie Williams, Guy Chambers
Duration: 3:40
B-side of the single 'Sexed Up'

We find Guy Chambers helping with the writing of this track with Irish sounds.

7

Greatest Hits

Release date:	18 October 2004
Producers:	Guy Chambers
Studios:	Abbey Road Studios, Air Lyndhurst Recording Studios, Angel Recording Studios, Battery Studios, Blah Street, Conway Studios, Jacobs Studios, Master Rock Studios, Matrix Maison Rouge Ltd, Sarm Hook End, Swanyard Studios, Wheeler End
Recordings:	1997–2004
Duration:	78:43
Label:	Chrysalis/EMI

Eight years after the start of his solo career, and at the origin of many hits, Robbie and his record company felt that it was time to offer a first compilation to celebrate the extraordinary progress made since his breakup with Take That. They therefore decided to release *Greatest Hits*, a compilation incorporating two unreleased tracks: 'Radio' and 'Misunderstood', recorded with his new partner in crime, Stephen Duffy. EMI Music did not lack the imagination to multiply the sales of the album: the record company varied the track list of the album according to the country.

When, for example, New Zealand benefited from a track list including the song 'Win Some Lose Some' (because the track was released as a promo single in this country), France was entitled to a track list including the French versions of 'Supreme', while Latin America released an edition that contained the Spanish version of 'Angels'.

And with each country releasing the album with two different covers, the release of the album turned into an exciting nightmare for collectors!

This compilation was also an opportunity for fans to get a taste of what the next album, also written with Stephen Duffy, was going to be, not only thanks to the 'Radio' and 'Misunderstood' singles, but also thanks to the many B-sides that accompanied them.

'Radio'

Writers: Robbie Williams, Stephen Duffy
Duration: 3:52
Released as a single: 4 October 2004
Charts: No. 1 in UK

When fans learned that Robbie has taken to working with Stephen Duffy, they were not sure what to expect. The two began working together in the summer of 2003, and the fruit of their collaboration emerged in the fall of 2004, with the release of Robbie's *Greatest Hits*, which featured two unreleased tracks: 'Radio' and 'Misunderstood'. Choosing Stephen Duffy for two singles that would accompany the release of a best of was therefore a risky bet, and obviously, the 'Rock DJ' performer had flair: 'Radio' was No. 1 in sales when it was released in the UK!

It is with a famous 'Ouch' expelled by Robbie that the 'Radio' track starts. This up-tempo track with electro sounds quickly reveals itself to be effective and dynamic. Here, Robbie opts for a deep voice. This serious tone inspires both blackness and virility.

This song is particularly interesting for its lyrics. Robbie talks about a male being, one that would have stolen everything from him. When you know the singer's personal life and what he has had to face in the past (and will face in the future), you quickly guess that Robbie is talking about the devil here. Torn between the angel and the demon, the singer describes in 'Radio' everything that this demon does to him: 'He's chosen my attic/I feel it in the static/He lives in my basement/And I can hardly face it'. The presence of the devil is even more evident in the music video. Dressed like a naval captain in a skimpy white suit, Robbie makes a series of grimaces in a neat choreography. Once again, he is surrounded exclusively by young women (and it would not be the last time) dressed as cheerleaders who perform particularly well-oiled choreography and impressive acrobatics. While the singer, dressed in white, represents good, the young women, dressed in black and heavily tattooed, embody evil. The stage takes place in a sort of huge hangar, and large curtains at the back suggest that you are on a concert stage, or rather in the rehearsal room. The pompoms and sequins dress the music video in a rather glamorous and sexy atmosphere. Further on, the video drifts into a more malicious universe: the demon in Robbie ends up surfacing, and the singer is no longer in a white suit, but shirtless. His now apparent tattoos let us say that the evil—symbolised by the tattoos of young women—ended up infecting the singer in turn. A tail (of an unknown animal) even pops out of the singer's butt (thanks for the special effects) and his face is distorted by the presence of the demon gnawing inside him. From the sight of the images, we understand that the demon is not only evil, he is also impulsive, driving his host to lust, as in the popular legends circulating about the devil.

In the end, 'Radio' was a success: the track reassured fans, excited the public, and gave incredible visibility to the *Greatest Hits*.

One can regret, however, that thereafter the song has not been often sung in concert. Despite being No. 1 in sales, Robbie would decide to sing it infrequently, just like another No. 1, 'Eternity', suffering a similar fate. On the contrary, some tracks, never released as a single, have been far more present on the set lists of concerts. This is the case, for example, with 'Monsoon', released on the album *Escapology* and featured very strongly on tours from 2002.

'Misunderstood'

Writers:	Robbie Williams, Stephen Duffy
Duration:	4:01
Released as a single:	6 December 2004
Charts:	No. 8 in UK

To further promote *Greatest Hits*, Robbie released a second single: 'Misunderstood'. Being a ballad, this track balances the scales with its predecessor, 'Radio', which was up-tempo. 'Misunderstood' is not just a *Greatest Hits* single, it is also the theme song for *Bridget Jones: The Edge of Reason*, which was released at the same time.

One could see a parallel between the character of Bridget Jones and that of Robbie: both are misunderstood. And that is what the song is about. On the one hand, Bridget, whose romantic adventures unsettle many, and on the other, Robbie, whose personal misadventures (drugs, alcohol) make him a touching and endearing personality.

Strange as it may sound, Robbie took inspiration from another movie to write this song; it was indeed inspired by the movie *Edward Scissorhands*, whose character was also misunderstood. Introduced by a harmonica, and accompanied by a guitar, 'Misunderstood' seduces us with its tenderness and melancholy.

In the music video, the singer, wearing an apple-green top, is told to explain himself in a police station. The video refers to one of the scenes in the film, in which Bridget finds herself in police custody. The video ends with a hint of humour, which calls back to his hit 'Millennium' (I will let you check this out for yourselves if you have not yet seen the video).

B-Sides Linked to *Greatest Hits*

'Northern Town'

Writers:	Robbie Williams, Stephen Duffy
Duration:	4:02

B-side of the single 'Radio'

Arguably one of Robbie's most simplistic and repetitive songs. The song mostly alternates the phrase 'Having good times' with 'In a Northern Town'. Only a few extra lines come in between from time to time, but the song essentially revolves between these two lines, all in a soaring atmosphere.

'1974'

Writers: Robbie Williams, Stephen Duffy
Duration: 4:22
B-side of the single 'Radio'

'1974' is Robbie's birth year—a normal thing to dedicate a song to. This track is a bit of a prelude to another song, 'The 80's', released on the *Rudebox* album. The song ends with: 'Child of the 80s/1974/Child of the 80s/1974'.

'Do Me Now (Demo)'

Writers: Robbie Williams, Boots Ottestad, Ian Bowden
Duration: 3:19
B-side of the single 'Misunderstood'

'Please, Please'

Writers: Robbie Williams, Stephen Duffy
Duration: 3:27
B-side of the single 'Misunderstood'

'(I Feel It) But I Can't Explain'

Writers: Robbie Williams, Stephen Duffy
Duration: 4:37
B-side of the single 'Misunderstood'

'Chemical Devotion'

Writers: Robbie Williams, Nick Lashley
Duration: 4:11
B-side of the single 'Misunderstood'

Another song where Robbie talks of drugs, and this time it is particularly explicit: 'It's in the laxative they're cutting in the cocaine baby/It's in the heroin, the ecstasy they're mixing lately'. 'Chemical Devotion' describes very well what Robbie's life was like when he was plagued by his demons and sins.

'The Postcard'

Writers: Stephen Duffy
Duration: 3:02
B-side of the single 'Misunderstood'

This song is interesting because it is a cover of Stephen Duffy, interpreted here by Robbie, and produced by Stephen. The beauty of the lyrics and the sweetness of Robbie's interpretation are especially memorable.

8

Intensive Care

Release date:	24 October 2005
Writers:	Robbie Williams, Stephen Duffy, Chris Heath
Producers:	Robbie Williams, Stephen Duffy
Studios:	Air Lyndhurst Recording Studios, East West Studio, Henson Studios, The Townhouse Studio
Recordings:	12 June 2003–May 2005
Duration:	53:02
Label:	Chrysalis/EMI

After the terrible breakup between Robbie and Guy Chambers, one can imagine that EMI Music was more than worried about the first album recorded without the singer's mentor. Three years had passed since *Escapology*, and Robbie was still required to release a further three studio albums to honour his deal signed in 2002. The origins of *Intensive Care* came alive in 2003, when the singer, then on a world tour, met Stephen Duffy. There was immediate chemistry, and from this encounter several dozen songs were created, many of which remain unpublished to this day.

Fans got their first glimpse of this fruitful collaboration in 2004, when the *Greatest Hits* was released, with the singles 'Radio' and 'Misunderstood'. But it was a year later, with the publication of *Intensive Care*, that they had the chance to discover all the facets of this musical partnership, both through the songs on the album and through that of the B-sides.

Intensive Care is an album title that conjures a sense of dread and worry. With this choice of title, you immediately feel that Robbie wanted to extend the exploration of a theme he had already addressed: that of darkness, doubts, and suffering. The stakes for Robbie were immense: to ensure that his success could survive the absence of Guy Chambers as well as establishing himself not only as a simple singer who writes songs and who puts his voice on a track, but also as a producer. Indeed, for the first time, Robbie was credited as the producer of his album, and so it was for all future albums he produced from 2005 onwards.

Physically, Robbie reverted to a wiser and more polished look than that of *Escapology*: shorter hair, a neat little lock, and a discreet earring. On the album cover—the photo of which is signed by Hamish Brown, his favourite photographer at the time—we see the presence of a guardian angel dressed in black (like the black of his outfit from the 'Angels' music video) as well as that of a demon dressed in blood red (the demon of 'Rock DJ' perhaps?). Finally, a mysterious symbol falsely tattooed under his index finger points to us.

'Ghosts'

Writers: Robbie Williams, Stephen Duffy
Duration: 3:42

The track that opens the album, 'Ghosts', starts in a very solemn way, which commands respect. Robbie opens the track as if he were opening a ceremony, and the first verse, filled with pride, makes us understand that it is very serious: 'Here I stand, victorious/The only man who made you come'. With the pun on the verb 'come', we suddenly change register to talk about something completely different: 'Gravity's calling/Don't go home/Where are we?'. Enough to destabilise more than one!

The song is a good introduction to the album, and it is with this song that he opens the promo concert he gave on 9 October 2005 in Berlin.

'Ghosts' refers to his former girlfriend, Nicole Appleton. When Robbie sings 'On the radio, she was that summer song', he is talking about the summer 2000 hit 'Pure Shores' by All Saints; this song was from *The Beach*'s movie soundtrack.

Fun fact: the first sentence of the song, 'Here I stand victorious, the only man who made you come', was written by his bodyguard, Duncan Pompey Wilkinson.

The theme of the song comes from the beliefs that Robbie developed from 2005. On numerous occasions, and especially in the years 2005–2008, the singer confessed his passion for surrealist phenomena: ghosts, aliens, etc. This theme comes up repeatedly.

'Tripping'

Writers: Robbie Williams, Stephen Duffy
Duration: 4:36
Single release date: 3 October 2005
Charts: No. 2 in UK

Reggae! What? Robbie does reggae? No, not really, but it is the sound that strikes us immediately when we first listen to 'Tripping'. As he knows so well how to do it, Robbie alternates here between deep and high voice—and that is what makes it so charming. Rare indeed are the singers who dare to push in the treble—no doubt in fear of putting on a feminine side that they would have a hard time assuming. Robbie, on the other hand, is very skilled at handling low and high voices with ease and variety; it is part of his talent. Although he is straight, he has never been afraid to have it both ways, sometimes probably just for fun, but also certainly out of curiosity or interest. The singer, who has never hidden his admiration for men like David Beckham, is a staunch defender of freedom. He who emancipated himself from the boy band Take That in which he was locked, who never refused any provocation, has always shown himself benevolent and full of admiration in front of same-sex couples.

Here in 'Tripping', the high-pitched voice is used to express not her femininity, but rather the intensity of her suffering: 'I've taken as much as I'm willing to take/ Why do you think we should suffer in silence/When a hearth is broken there's nothing to break'. It is also the occasion to appreciate again some verses sung in rap: 'When you think we're lost, we're exploring/What you think is work because I'm adoring/You don't want the truth, truth is boring'.

In the music video, Robbie finds himself in a nightmare. He is notably seen running in the rooms of a hotel whose green corridors are similar to those in the clip for 'Sexed Up', released two years earlier. Immersed in the universe of *Alice in Wonderland*, Robbie meets many characters, each equally distressing. Among the anxieties, we have the car's speedometer which gets stuck on mileage 21,886, an elevator that gets stuck on the eighteenth floor. It all ends in a labyrinth, a place that was found many years later in another music video for the singer.

'Make Me Pure'

Writers:	Robbie Williams, Stephen Duffy, Chris Heath
Duration:	4:33
Single release date:	14 November 2005
Charts:	No. 15 in Netherlands

When *Intensive Care* was released in 2005, the public was still used to physical singles, and digital singles were not yet readily accessible. But already, at this time, the singer understood that he had been forced to follow the trend. He decided to release his very first digital single: 'Make Me Pure'. Even though, at the time, fans did not really consider it a full single due to the lack of physical support, 'Make Me Pure' is indeed a single: it has a cover (digitised), his own music video, and he was even squeezed on promotional media.

'Make Me Pure' is filled with simplicity—or purity, I should say. The acoustic-style track highlights Robbie's new band, vocals, and backing vocals. But let us talk about the choirs; after an intro that combines instruments and the singer's voice, the song gently introduces the presence of the choirs. As the song progresses, their strength intensifies, and then takes off quickly, gospel style, until reaching a power that paralyzes you on the spot—not a paralysis in the form of pain, a paralysis that grabs all your emotions and takes you with it. Listening to the choirs, you are carried away, and you fly. Robbie then shows himself as a conductor directing delicious tortures. Who can dream of better?

'Spread Your Wings'

Writers: Robbie Williams, Stephen Duffy
Duration: 3:50

'Advertising Space'

Writers: Robbie Williams, Stephen Duffy
Duration: 4:37
Single release date: 2 December 2005
Charts: No. 8 in UK

After the very original 'Tripping' and the acoustic track 'Make Me Pure', Robbie serves us here a magnificent ride with 'Advertising Space'. He takes us here in a moment of nostalgia, where sad events of the '70s, like the Watergate scandal and the Vietnam War, are called to mind: 'A special agent for the man/Water gates and Vietnam', as well as another more recent sad event: 'I saw you standing at the gate/When Marlon Brando passed away'. The poetry that emerges then tends to embellish and idealise the past.

In the music video, the singer pays a brilliant tribute to Elvis Presley. Dressed in leather, he tenderly embodies an Elvis fan who sings in old cabarets. The video ends with the image of his 'Elvis Grant Me Serenity' tattoo, which was done several years earlier.

Robbie had paid homage to Elvis in the past. His most glaring tribute dates to 2002, during his live DVD *The Robbie Williams Show*, when the aesthetics and style echoed entirely, with only a few details, those of the *68 Comeback Special*. Like Elvis in 1968, Robbie had chosen in 2002 to make his comeback with a show broadcast only on the small screen.

Elvis Presley's influence on Robbie's career recurs regularly, sometimes explicitly, sometimes much more subtly.

'Please Don't Die'

Writers: Robbie Williams, Stephen Duffy
Duration: 4:47

This track is arguably one of Robbie's most touching songs, and listening to the lyrics is sure to bring you to tears. In two sentences, your heart stops dead: 'And if you die before I leave/What on earth becomes of me/Look around there's no one here/To love me and hold me'.

However, this track does not fall into the cutesy lament one might have imagined. Although similar in nature to a ballad, the song nevertheless claims an incredible energy, far from the sad clichés that these lyrics would suggest. It contains an unsuspected strength, full of optimism. The mid-tempo rhythm and the liveliness of the strings and percussions have something to warm our hearts. The song recalls the loss of a loved one, while providing instrumental and vocal consolation. The strength is felt especially in this passage: 'Maybe I've been away too long/I know I'm not always right but is that wrong/They say there's nothing I can do/But talk to strangers and wait for you'.

'Your Gay Friend'

Writers: Robbie Williams, Stephen Duffy
Duration: 3:22

'Sin Sin Sin'

Writers: Robbie Williams, Stephen Duffy, Chris Heath
Duration: 4:09
Single release date: 22 May 2006
Charts: No. 22 in UK

'Sin Sin Sin' was the very first track Robbie and Stephen Duffy recorded together on 12 June 2003. This single is not Robbie's best known. Released at the very beginning of his world tour in 2006, the track undoubtedly suffered from the shadow generated by this event. However, the track benefits from a good dynamic: music mixing electro and strings, accompanied by a heady chorus: 'Sin sin sin/Look where we've been/And where we are tonight'.

The song gains momentum quickly, especially in concert and in the accompanying music video. In it, Robbie plays the role of a cult guru surrounded by women—a situation that immediately makes you smile when you know his reputation at the time. What makes Robbie successful is also his failure, or at least his risk of failure.

The reason he is so successful is that fans appreciate his demons (alcohol, drugs, weight gain), provocations, and boy band charm. But paradoxically, we also know that dark thoughts may have pushed Robbie to the precipice. In the grip of his doubts, anxieties, and discomfort, how many times has he found himself on the edge of the abyss? Fortunately, he always managed to escape, like a phoenix rising from the ashes.

'Random Acts of Kindness'

Writers: Robbie Williams, Stephen Duffy
Duration: 4:16

'The Trouble With Me'

Writers: Robbie Williams, Stephen Duffy
Duration: 4:20

'A Place to Crash'

Writers: Robbie Williams, Stephen Duffy
Duration: 4:34

King of Bloke and Bird

Writers: Robbie Williams, Stephen Duffy
Duration: 6:10

B-Sides Linked to *Intensive Care*

'Meet the Stars'

Writers: Robbie Williams, Stephen Duffy
Duration: 4:27
B-side of the single 'Tripping'

This song is done in the electro style, with a dreamlike atmosphere. It represents well the musical orientation taken by Robbie between 2004 and 2006 with Stephen Duffy.

'Bag Full of Silly'

Writers: Robbie Williams, Stephen Duffy
Duration: 4:15
B-side of the single 'Tripping'

'Family Coach'

Writers: Stephen Duffy
Duration: 4:50
B-side of the single 'Advertising Space'

'Twist'

Writers: Robbie Williams
Duration: 4:50
B-side of the single 'Advertising Space'

This is an instrumental track. Robbie does not sing on this song.

'Don't Say No'

Writers: Robbie Williams, Stephen Duffy
Duration: 4:28
B-side of the single 'Advertising Space'

'Overture for Berlin'

Writers: Stephen Duffy
Duration: 3:37
B-side of the single 'Advertising Space'

This is the second instrumental track (or rather almost fully instrumental as the singer's voice is briefly heard); it is taken from the single 'Advertising Space'. This track was composed to be broadcast as an intro to the Berlin concert that took place to launch the promotion of the *Intensive Care* album. As a result, this track was only broadcast once, but it was particularly successful and was a very good way to introduce the concert.

The track starts with a sound like the sonar of submarine, before building to end on a set of violins and percussions. The dynamics of the piece are set up quickly and involve choirs. Where the track becomes brilliant is that it manages to combine very classic sounds (strings and percussion) with much more modern sounds (we hear in the background sounds of rap and hip hop). After a slight slowdown to hold the listener's attention, Robbie's voice is heard on just two sentences: 'And it looks like we could have made it, baby' and 'Me and You'. These two sentences are in fact taken from the song 'Ghosts', a song which was performed just after 'Overture for Berlin' on the evening of this concert.

The piece ends in apotheosis, with the choirs taking over again, to allow the arrival of the singer on stage.

'Our Love'

Writers: Robbie Williams, Stephen Duffy
Duration: 4:12
B-side of the single 'Sin Sin Sin'

'Don't Stop Talking'

Writers: Robbie Williams, Stephen Duffy
Duration: 5:12

In 2006, Robbie signed a deal with Sony Ericsson, to promote the release of the Sony Ericsson W800i mobile. On this occasion, the brand released a special edition, in the colours of Robbie (the design took up the logo of the singer, as well as the artwork of the album *Intensive Care*). To reinforce the promotion of this mobile, an unreleased song by the singer, 'Don't Stop Talking', was available only in digital format inside the phone. Subsequently, the song was released in CD format, on CD 3 of the *In and Out of Consciousness* compilation, which features mostly B-sides by Robbie. Releasing a song whose title is 'Don't Stop Talking' to promote a mobile was rather well done.

9

Rudebox

Release date:	23 October 2006
Writers:	Robbie Williams, Kelvin Andrews, Danny Spencer, Bill Laswell, Carl Aiken, Williams Collins, Sly Dunbar, Robbie Shakespeare, Lewis Taylor, Manu Chao, Anouk Khelifa, Neil Tennant, Chris Lowe, Chris Heath, Stephen Duffy, Jerry Meehan, Brandon Christy, Craig Russo, Jo Callis, Phil Oakey, Adrian Wright, My Robot Friend, Antony Genn
Producers:	Soul Mekanik, Mark Ronson, Pet Shop Boys, Brandon Christy, Craig Russo, William Orbit, Joey Negro, Jerry Meehan
Studios:	Z Records Studio, Guerilla Studios, The Actor's Studios, Chillout Studios, Chung King Studios, Wendy House Studios, Sarm Studios
Recordings:	November 2005–August 2006
Duration:	74:44
Label:	Chrysalis/EMI

In the summer of 2006, Robbie was the king of the world; by this point in his career, he had already sold millions of albums, won numerous awards, and broken a series of records. Nothing seemed to stop him anymore. From 1997 to 2005, the singer released one record per year (if you count the compilation *The Ego Has Landed*), and as a result, his ubiquity in the media for more than eight years without interruption since the beginning of his solo career started to generate nervousness, annoyance, and jealousy. Perhaps it was time for the media to seize every opportunity to bring down the star they have time admired in the past, and the *Rudebox* album undoubtedly represented this golden opportunity that they did not want to pass up.

While touring the world, Robbie had the arrogance to release a new album, which represents both a new musical direction and a new golden nugget that only the most knowledgeable and sensitive fans will appreciate. When the very confusing debut single 'Rudebox'—of the same title as the album—was unveiled to the press, the singer faced tough criticism. The press, with tabloids leading, attacked Robbie even before the single was released to the public. The goal was clear: to nip Robbie's new single in the bud. We witnessed a real execution. While the singer was still on tour when the track was released, he found himself unable to react to the affront. From then on, it was impossible for him to retaliate, and the album *Rudebox* found itself doomed even before its release. Worse still, the fans were not ready for this new musical experience, and some of them let themselves be convinced by the media and the album never managed to restore its letters of nobility.

And yet, what a mistake! The *Rudebox* album is one of the singer's best, and it contains many nuggets. No one is quite sure how Robbie found the time to record this album, which features no less than sixteen tracks, five of which were released as singles. Indeed, the album was recorded between November 2005 and August 2006, a period already very busy for the singer since he was at the same time promoting the album *Intensive Care* and on the Close Encounters Tour, one of his biggest tours!

Rudebox is simply amazing! Between the first track, the famous 'Rudebox', with electro rap trends, the very elegant 'Lovelight', the very glamorous 'She's Madonna', the subtle 'The Actor', the festive and sexy 'Kiss Me', and even the heavenly 'Summertime', there is an evident mix of genres, with rap, electro, dance, and pop coming together in this unexpected, experimental, and *avant-garde* opus.

Still busy with the end of his tour, the singer was unable to promote the album. But he was undoubtedly also discouraged by the relentlessness of the press towards him.

Fortunately, the album, despite suffering from a bad reputation and a glaring lack of promotion, still ended up as No. 1 in sales the week it was released, and the much-feared *NME* magazine wrote: '"*Rudebox*" is the best thing he's ever put his name to'.

'Rudebox (Single)'

Writers:	Robbie Williams, Kelvin Andrews Mould, Daniel Spencer Mould, Bill Laswell, Carl Edmund Aiken, William Collins, Sly Dunbar, Robert Shakespeare
Duration:	4:45
Single release date:	4 September 2006
Charts:	No. 4 in UK

Despite the criticism from the press, despite the commercial failure of the single, 'Rudebox' is one of my favourite Robbie tracks. This song is a gem, and I will prove it to you.

First of all, it is a breath of fresh air that blows in the singer's career. With audiences accustomed to Britpop, rock, or swing tracks, 'Rudebox' wakes up Robbie fans who have fallen asleep to clichés. This is electro-rap, a genre he had not yet tackled. It is also an effective dance track, very simple on the instrumental level, but very rich in terms of lyrics.

With humour, the singer uses the word 'Rudebox' in every way, and lets the listener guess what he is talking about: 'Do the rudebox/Shake your rudebox/Do the rudebox/Shake your rudebox'.

By linking rap verses and frenzied beats, 'Rudebox', coupled with its music video, is aimed at fans of street art and dance, and is defined as a manual for a successful choreography with perfection. Each line of the song deserves to be cited in this book because it is literary genius. Each sentence flows together with such flexibility and ease; one wonders how this track could not have been written before. We especially enjoy when we discover how Robbie juggles here with the words: 'OK then, back to spaceship/Take both pills, fuck the Matrix/Jack those Jills, shake your Playtex/Rock three stripes, not the Asics/A-D-I-D-A-S old school, 'cause it's the best'.

'Viva Life on Mars'

Writers: Robbie Williams, Kelvin Andrews Mould, Daniel Spencer Mould
Duration: 4:51

This country-style track is a glimpse into Robbie's passion for UFOs from 2006. In addition to the *Close Encounters of the Third Kind* theme used on his 2006 world tour, the singer continues to explore this theme in this song 'Viva Life on Mars'.

Curiously, the song includes a line from George Michael's famous hit 'I Want Your Sex': 'Love is natural, love is good. Not everybody does it, but everybody should'.

The singer also references a Pet Shop Boys hit, 'West End Girls', when he sings 'Free yourself from liberation, from Lake Geneva to the Freeland Station'.

Later, in 2008, Robbie became obsessed with his passion for UFOs.

'Lovelight'

Writers: Lewis Taylor
Duration: 4:02
Single release date: 13 November 2006
Charts: No. 8 in UK

Definitely one of Robbie's most amazing singles. Although the high-pitched sound of his voice has been glimpsed in older songs before, this is the first time he has applied this tone to an entire song. By the way, the first time I listened to 'Lovelight', I did not recognise his voice.

'Lovelight' is, in fact, a cover (as there are many on the *Rudebox* album): the song comes from Lewis Taylor, who released it in 2003. Produced by the very talented Mark Ronson, it was the music video that seduced fans. Shot in Vienna, Austria, during the 2006 tour, in a music academy, the video plunges the viewer into a glamorous, dark, and sexy atmosphere. Robbie, dressed first in a black military costume (which is reminiscent of the white costume from the single 'Radio' released two years earlier), then in a black shirt, embodies a new kind of army leader, surrounded by a troop with strict military movements. In this post-war setting, we can see a fictitious flag in the background, which could be likened to that of a dictatorship. In fact, the only dictatorship in question here is that of fashion, and the singer seems to be the leader.

The style of the video is very reminiscent of the aesthetics of George Michael's music videos. We may only regret the undoubtedly too dark images of the video, preventing us from grasping all the subtleties it contains.

'Bongo Bong and Je Ne T'aime Plus'

Writers: Manu Chao
Duration: 4:48

'She's Madonna'

Writers: Robbie Williams, Neil Tennant, Chris Lowe
Duration: 4:16
Single release date: 5 March 2007
Charts: No. 16 in UK

When this single was released in 2007, it was no secret that many fans were hoping for a duet between Robbie and the Queen of Pop. While this duet never happened (and maybe never will), it was not unusual for them to write a song about Madonna.

But was the single 'She's Madonna' directly dedicated to Madonna? Not really. In fact, here Madonna is not mentioned as a person, nor even as a singer, actress, or Queen of Pop, but as a symbol of celebrity. Indeed, as the lyrics point out: 'I love you baby/But face it she's Madonna/No man on earth/Could say that he don't want her'. Robbie is not talking about her talent or her music, but about her power; more specifically, the power she has over men. In this song, Madonna is seen as a symbol of seduction and fascination.

From then on, in 'She's Madonna', the singer is seen as a trophy that any straight man would love to take home: 'But all I wanna do/Is take Madonna home'. However, the singer's personality is not completely erased. He sings with a certain accuracy: 'She's got to be obscene to be believed/That's her routine not what she means to me'.

'She's Madonna' was also Robbie's opportunity to call on the Pet Shop Boys again. Having previously featured Neil Tennant on his single 'No Regrets' in 1998, the British duo returned to provide backing vocals.

On the music video side, the song takes on a whole new dimension. After a long intro in which Robbie, disguised as a drag queen, answers journalists' questions, the video takes us to the artist's dressing room, where he changes into a more masculine outfit. Dressed in white, he takes on a similar appearance to that of John Travolta in *Saturday Night Fever* to take to the stage of a cabaret whose spectators are all drag queens! So everything is reversed: the drag queen has become a heterosexual man, and the audience has been replaced by depressed drag queens.

At the end of the day, 'She's Madonna' was undoubtedly Robbie's gayest track: the evocation of a gay icon, the presence of the Pet Shop Boys as well as that of a drag queen make this track a funny and subtle tribute to gay culture.

'Keep On'

Writers: Robbie Williams, Stephen Duffy, Chris Heath
Duration: 4:19

'Good Doctor'

Writers: Robbie Williams, Jerry Meehan
Duration: 3:17

'The Actor'

Writers: Robbie Williams, Brandon Christy, Craig Russo
Duration: 4:06

One of my favourite Robbie songs, and arguably one of the most unfairly underestimated of his career. A bell rings and the voice of a director is heard: this is how the song 'The Actor' begins. Here, Robbie uses the spoken-sung technique to recite his first verses. A female voice (Marsha Thomason) accompanies it between each sentence.

Strange as it may sound, even though the female voice is perfectly audible, and not part of the backing vocals, it is not a duet, or even a featuring. This is a Robbie song.

The structure is simple: 'The Actor' works like a dialogue between a director (Robbie) who makes a series of cold and cynical statements and an actress (Marsha Thomason is actually an actress in real life) who, for her part, lists another series of confessions, not as if responding to Robbie, but if the song allows us to hear the actress's inner voice.

'The Actor' is one of the singer's most electro tracks. We notice that the principle of vocoder is applied to his voice on the chorus: 'I don't know where you begin/I end, we start/Again'. Despite the acidity and coldness of the atmosphere, the alternation of the singer's metallic voice with the actress's sexy voice creates a kind of exciting and gripping game.

Then the genius of this song is amplified in the second part, when Robbie decides to imitate the style of the famous Madonna's 'Vogue'. The Queen of Pop lists a very long series of actor names: 'Greta Garbo and Monroe/Dietrich and DiMaggio/Marlon Brando, Jimmy Dean/On the cover of a magazine/Grace Kelly, Harlow, Jean/Picture of a beauty queen/Gene Kelly, Fred Astaire/Ginger Rogers, dance on air/They had style, they had grace/Rita Hayworth gave good face/Lauren, Katherine, Lana too/Bette Davis, we love you'.

Robbie had the idea to do the same, in his own way, with an equally similar enumeration: 'Monroe, (Monroe)/Barrymore, (Barrymore)/Mansfield, (Mansfield)/D-d-d-d-Dame d-Dame d-Dame Judi Dench, (Judi Dench)/Madonna Ritchie, (Ritchie)/Ritchie, Ritchie, Ritchie/Streep, Close'. Note that only Marilyn Monroe is mentioned in both songs, and we also note that Robbie himself quotes Madonna, making 'Vogue' a Russian doll that 'The Actor' would contain. Robbie appends the last name Ritchie to the first name Madonna—the singer was still married to Guy Ritchie at the time of writing and publishing this song.

Finally, the song ends with this line: 'In the future/Everybody will be anonymous for fifteen minutes'. This line echoes Andy Warhol's famous quote: 'In the future, everyone will be world-famous for 15 minutes'. Robbie was very impressed by this quote, since it is present at the beginning of the music video of 'Something Beautiful'. Three years after 'Something Beautiful', Robbie cynically predicts that in the future, people will do anything to have even a few minutes of anonymity.

'The Actor' is therefore both a cinematic response to Madonna's very fashionable 'Vogue' and a nod to the famous quote from Andy Warhol, two gay icons from Pop Art.

'Never Touch That Switch'

Writers: Kelvin Andrews Mould, Daniel Spencer Mould
Duration: 2:47

'Louise'

Writers: The Human League
Duration: 4:46

'We're the Pet Shop Boys'

Writers: My Robot Friend
Duration: 4:57

'Kiss Me'

Writers: Stephen Duffy
Duration: 3:18

Here is a particularly fresh track. Robbie is best known for his pop, rock, and swing tracks, but 'Kiss Me' is the perfect example of the electro dance track produced by the King of Entertainment.

If you want to have a blast and have a good time, this is the song for you: light, efficient, and energetic—a dance song as we like it.

Note that a female voice, provided here by Katherine Ellis, a chorister specialising in electro and house music, says a few words in French pronounced in a sulphurous manner: '*Oh c'étai*', '*Toi et moi*', and '*Jamais, jamais*'. Listening to this track is also interesting as Robbie's vocals come close to the timbre he had in the '95–96 years on some songs or demos.

'The 80's'

Writers: Robbie Williams, Jerry Meehan
Duration: 4:18

When Robbie promoted this song, he asked his fans to enter a contest: the goal was to make a music video for this song. Many fans participated, and the winning music video featured a teenager filmed in his bedroom.

'The 80's' is a rap track, arguably the singer's first fully rap track. It takes us into the nostalgia of the '80s, and the music accompanying Robbie's voice reproduces that feeling of melancholy well.

'The 90's'

Writers: Robbie Williams, Jerry Meehan
Duration: 5:34

'Summertime'

Writers: Robbie Williams, Anthony Genn
Duration: 5:41

'Dickhead'

Writers: Robbie Williams, Jerry Meehan
Duration: 4:09

B-Sides Linked to *Rudebox*

'Lonestar Rising'

Writers: Robbie Williams, Kelvin Andrews Mould, Daniel Spencer Mould
Duration: 3:52
B-side of the single 'Rudebox'

'Lonestar Rising' fits well with the single 'Rudebox', of which it is the B-side. We discover the vocoded voice of the singer, whose sentences alternate with male choruses tirelessly repeating 'Bah-um'.

'Mess Me Up'

Writers: Soul Mekanik
Duration: 5:12
B-side of the single 'Lovelight'

We find here male choirs, similar to those of the single 'Rudebox'. In this experimental and entertaining song, Robbie plays with words, accompanied by a more or less robotic voice. Do not attach too much importance to the lyrics.

'In and Out of Love'

Writers: Robbie Williams, Kelvin Andrews Mould, Daniel Spencer Mould
Duration: 4:18

This song is not a B-side but was probably recorded during the *Rudebox* sessions. It was offered to fans at Christmas 2007.

10

Reality Killed the Video Star

Release date:	9 November 2009
Writers:	Robbie Williams, Kelvin Andrews, Daniel Spencer, Richard Scott, Scott Ralph, Don Black, Brandon Christy, Craig Russo, Guy Chambers, Chaz Jankel, Andy Stubbs, Jonathan Hand, Stephen Cadman, Paul Beard, Fil Eisler, Françoise Hardy
Producers:	Trevor Horn
Studios:	Sarm Studios, Sarm West Coast, Capitol Studios, Angel Recording Studios
Recordings:	September 2008–August 2009
Duration:	51:30
Label:	Chrysalis/Virgin/EMI

When Robbie decided to release *Reality Killed the Video Star*, he came out of an almost three-year hiatus: the single 'She's Madonna' was released in the spring of 2007, then the first single from the new album, 'Bodies', premiered in October 2009. However, at the time of the release of this new opus, nobody knew how the public would react.

First, although the previous tour (the Close Encounters Tour in 2006) was a huge success, the album that was released during that tour, *Rudebox*, was a failure, especially in terms of image. Plus, 2007 and 2008 were not painless for Robbie; in a few months, the singer had gone through detoxification and weight gain. The fans were lost, and the singer had undoubtedly lost confidence in himself.

The stakes for Robbie were therefore high: he had to make his comeback and reassure his fans, seduce the critics, please the public, and regain his self-confidence. For his new album, Robbie called for the first time the producer Trevor Horn, to whom we owe the Buggles hit 'Video Killed the Radio Star' in 1979. In the blink of an eye, Robbie was inspired to name his new opus after this, replacing the words 'video' with 'reality' and 'radio' with 'video'.

This choice of song names was smart. It was thirty years after Trevor's famous hit, and Robbie felt times had changed. Just like the famous 'In the future everybody will be famous for 15 minutes' that Robbie transformed into 'In the future everybody will be anonymous for 15 minutes', the singer updated Trevor's hit by creating a version 2.0 of the concept. If in 1979, the emergence of the music video (the golden age of which was in the '80s/'90s with the arrival of MTV) certainly overshadowed radio, Robbie estimated that thirty years later, it is reality (reality TV? Or quite simply reality) which in turn overshadows the music video. This was a fairly relevant view, since after 2009, the development of social networks has relegated video clips, physical release, and even reality TV to the rank of outdated.

Even though 'Bodies', the first single, failed to reach No. 1 in sales, it nevertheless climbed to second place, and in terms of images, this single symbolises the singer's big comeback. The honour is safe: 'Bodies' is efficient, hard-hitting, and gives Robbie a sense of self-confidence—a confidence that he wanted to confirm the following year, without a doubt, when he decided to go on tour with Take That instead of offering a solo tour to his audience; the latter had to wait until 2013 to finally find the King of Entertainment on stage.

Although Robbie was still not reconciled with Guy Chambers at the time, the album contains a track written by the latter, 'Blasphemy'. In fact, this song was written in 2002, during the recording of *Escapology* and just before their breakup.

'Morning Sun'

Writers:	Robbie Williams, Kelvin Andrews Mould, Daniel Spencer Mould, Richard Scott, Scott Ralph, Don Black
Duration:	4:06
Single release date:	8 March 2010
Charts:	No. 45 in UK

When *Reality Killed the Video Star* came out, the track 'Morning Sun' was billed as Robbie's new 'Angels'. It is true that, at the first listen, everything is done to entice. Once again, the singer delivers a superb ride. After an intro on harmonica, piano, and violin, we are treated to superb lyrics, which inspire poetry and comfort, triggered by the magnificent 'How do you rate the morning sun?' The singer continues with a very nice play on words: 'How many stars would you give to the moon?'

In the music video, Robbie plays a new character: that of an astronaut. This should come as no surprise when you consider that since at least 2006 he had developed a passion for space, aliens, and paranormal phenomena. It was therefore obvious that he was devoting a video to this new passion. The video alternates images from NASA and close-up shots on the singer's face.

When Michael Jackson died on 25 June 2009, Robbie said he wrote and recorded a song in his homage. It was 'Morning Sun'. The track is written with the help of Don Black, author of several songs for the credits of James Bond. However, when the album was released, Robbie admitted that despite his intention, the song is not about Michael, but himself.

Unfortunately, the single was a real commercial failure. It only ranked No. 45 in the UK Singles Chart, one of Robbie's worst performances on the charts.

'Bodies'

Writers:	Robbie Williams, Brandon Christy, Craig Russo
Duration:	4:03
Single release date:	12 October 2009
Charts:	No. 2 in UK

The title of the song alone is intriguing: 'Bodies'. This word can suggest both death and sex—something to confuse the fans. But a reading of the lyrics suggests that we are moving more towards death: 'Bodies in the cemetery/And that's the way it's gonna be'. Everyone remembers the single 'Angels', and especially its music video, which had a very religious vibe—dressed in black, Robbie sang a song with a prayer tune. By discovering the lyrics of 'Bodies', we find a rather mysterious religious theme: 'And your Jesus really died for me/I guess Jesus really tried for me'. While there is no doubt that the lyrics have a strong theme, it would be unwise to put any specific meaning to this song. The singer will admit himself later, in October 2010: 'Who knows what I was going on about? I was fucking stoned'.

In fact, when you listen to the track, it sounds more like Robbie had fun playing with the word 'Bodies' in order to get dynamic and energetic verses. However, in another interview, the singer revealed some information about the song. According to him, the sentence 'And your Jesus really died for me' was written to refer to the 2003 Iraq War, when George Bush sent people to die in a war in Jesus's name. For Robbie, the death of Jesus cannot be used to justify a war, nor to send people to die in his name.

In contrast, the expression 'God save me rejection from my reflection/I want perfection' refers to problems related to anorexia, bulimia, and people who are not satisfied with their body. In reality, it should be understood that the song 'Bodies' is a kind of definition that one could find in a dictionary: the singer explains in music, all the meanings, or all the themes to which the word 'Bodies' can be attached. To better understand the origin of the song 'Bodies', we must refer to an interview given by Guy Chambers in 2019. In this interview, the producer explains: 'He's completely obsessed with words—lyrics are his passion, he loves rap battles and things like that—and I'm very passionate about the more musical composition, production side'.

Although Guy Chambers was neither involved in the writing nor in the production of this track, here we recognise the robot portrait of the writer Robbie: he is completely obsessed with words, and this is one of the singer's recipes or secrets. Some of its titles tracks are so well chosen that they could be likened to the names of products that a marketing team would be responsible for promoting: 'Bodies', 'Millennium', 'Supreme', 'Feel', 'Angels'—so many words which have been also chosen later like street names for his hometown. In 2015, the city of Stoke-on-Trent indeed decided to rename several of its streets based on the songs of the native child: Angels Way, Candy Lane, Supreme Street. Admittedly, it is much easier to wear than names like Thriller Avenue, Purple Rain Street or Like a Virgin Boulevard.

In the music video, the singer made it big. Filmed in the middle of the Mojave Desert in the United States, we see Robbie using or referring to several means of transport: a motorcycle, an all-terrain car, an aeroplane, and a 4×4.

The video works like an allegory: after crossing the desert he has just experienced between 2007 and 2009, the singer is back in a desert. He is seen shaving, as if making his comeback, as well as fixing a motorcycle (nod to the 'Angels' music video by the way), which he ends up riding. The video, directed by Vaughan Arnell, echoes another video of the singer, shot by the same director: 'Supreme'. Indeed, here, Vaughan Arnell uses the technique of split-screen, which consists of cutting the image into several small images: a technique widely used in films of the '60s and '70s, and that we find in the clip by 'Supreme'. On his journey in the desert, he meets Ayda Field, who, in real life, became his wife a year later. The video ends with a very astonishing scene: the singer is in an aircraft graveyard. If the planes here symbolise the famous bodies of which the singer speaks, some will have seen here a reference to 9/11. Standing on an aeroplane wing, Robbie dances elegantly and delivers the last verses of the track.

Musically, the song is particularly effective: it alternates between persistent electro sounds and incisive violins with similar energy to that of thunderclaps, all associated with an enumeration of powerful sentences. The word 'Bodies' resonates like stab wounds the singer strikes at his listener, and yet, the track almost never came out as a single. Trevor Horn, the producer, explained: 'Initially we had no intention of releasing it as a first single at all, but I tried to replace electronic instruments with real instruments, and suddenly it blew everyone away, and Robbie has adored it!'

'You Know Me'

Writers:	Robbie Williams, Candy Flip, Kelvin Andrews Mould, Daniel Spencer Mould, Françoise Hardy
Duration:	4:21
Single release date:	4 December 2009
Charts:	No. 6 in UK

For 'You Know Me', Robbie samples the song 'Voilà' by Françoise Hardy. This love song seems to take on a very light tone, and very close to caricature: 'Since you went away, my heart breaks everyday/You don't know 'cause you're not there'. Musically, we are moving towards an eccentric style inspired by Elton John, an eccentricity that can also be found in the clip where the singer is disguised as a rabbit. We are the opposite of the very serious 'Angels', 'Feel', or 'Morning Sun'. The choice of this song as the second single from the album is quite surprising. About as surprising as 'Something Beautiful', which is similar in style to Elton's, as a single from the album *Escapology*.

'Blasphemy'

Writers: Robbie Williams, Guy Chambers
Duration: 4:18

'Do You Mind'

Writers: Robbie Williams, Kelvin Andrews Mould, Daniel Spencer Mould, Chaz Jankel
Duration: 4:06

'Last Days of Disco'

Writers: Robbie Williams, Kelvin Andrews Mould, Daniel Spencer Mould
Duration: 4:50

This track was used for the trailer of the concert—at the Roundhouse in London—which marked the great return of Robbie, in 2009, after three years of absence. The choice of this elegant song, including sounds crossing electro and disco, is completely consistent when we hear this sentence: 'Don't call it a comeback/We'll hold an event in here'.

'Somewhere'

Writers: Robbie Williams, Kelvin Andrews Mould, Daniel Spencer Mould, Andy Stubbs, Jonathan Hand
Duration: 1:01

'Deceptacon'

Writers: Robbie Williams, Kelvin Andrews Mould, Richard Scott, Scott Ralph
Duration: 5:01

'Starstruck'

Writers: Robbie Williams, Kelvin Andrews Mould, Daniel Spencer Mould, Paul Beard
Duration: 5:21

If we only listened to certain verses of this song, we would think that George Michael is the singer! Robbie here adopts the same dark voice as George in certain passages. Musically, we also find the trademark of the 'Faith' singer: the mid-tempo rhythm, the electro style, and the very feminine choirs.

'Difficult for Weirdos'

Writers: Robbie Williams, Kelvin Andrews Mould, Daniel Spencer Mould
Duration: 4:30

This song imitates the style of the Pet Shop Boys to perfection. She combines classical instruments and electro sounds, carried by a voice as soft as velvet. Once again, a great elegance in the orchestration, equivalent to that which Neil Tenant and Chris Lowe can produce.

'Superblind'

Writers: Robbie Williams, Fil Eisler
Duration: 4:46

'Won't Do That'

Writers: Robbie Williams, Kelvin Andrews Mould, Daniel Spencer Mould, Richard Scott, Scott Ralph
Duration: 3:39

'Morning Sun (Reprise)'

Writers: Robbie Williams, Kelvin Andrews Mould, Daniel Spencer Mould, Richard Scott, Scott Ralph, Don Black
Duration: 1:23

'Arizona'

Writers: Robbie Williams, Kelvin Andrews Mould, Daniel Spencer Mould
Duration: 5:38

B-Sides Linked to *Reality Killed the Video Star*

'Elastik'

Writers: Robbie Williams, Kelvin Andrews Mould, Daniel Spencer Mould, Richard Scott
Duration: 4:36
B-side of the single 'Morning Sun'

Written with the help of his electro team (Kelvin Andrews Mould, Daniel Spencer Mould) 'Elastik' has quite retro connotations, associated with a slight disco feeling. We find ourselves a little halfway between the style of the *Rudebox* album and that of *Reality Killed the Video Star*.

11

In and Out of Consciousness

Release date:	8 October 2010
Writers:	Robbie Williams, Guy Chambers, Ashley Hamilton, Bill Laswell, Billy Morrison, Boots Ottestad, Brandon Christy, Carl Aiken, Carson Parks, Cary Baylis, Chris Heath, Chris Lowe, Craig Russo, Daniel Pierre, Daniel Spencer Mould, Desmond Child, Dino Fekaris, Don Black, Duncan Bridgeman, Ekundayo Paris, Eliot Kennedy, Eric Bazilian, Françoise Hardy, Freddie Perren, Gary Barlow, Gary Nuttall, George Michael, Glen Ballard, Jamie Catto , Jerry Jeff Walker, John Baker, John Barry, Jon Brookes, Karl Wallinger, Kelvin Andrews Mould, Leslie Bricusse, Lewis Taylor, Martin Blunt, Martin Page, Maxi Jazz, Mike Ward, Morrison, Neil Tennant, Nelson Pigford, Nigel Butler, Ray Davies, Richard Scott, Rob Collins, Robbie Shakespeare, Scott Ralph, Sly Dunbar, Stephen Duffy, Tim Burgess, William Collins
Producers:	Robbie Williams, Trevor Horn, Guy Chambers, Steve Power, Pet Shop Boys, Mark Ronson, Soul Mekanik, Gary Barlow, Stephen Duffy, Stephen Hague
Studios:	Capitol Studios, The Village Recorders, The Garage, Ocean Studios
Recordings:	1993–June 2010
Label:	Chrysalis/Virgin/EMI

In 2010, Robbie celebrated twenty years of his career, including both with Take That and solo. This created an opportunity for him to release a new compilation, six years after *Greatest Hits*, but to avoid offering a pale copy of *Greatest Hits*, EMI Music—which was about to be acquired by Universal—decided to release a totally different concept. This time not only were the songs listed in reverse chronological order from newest to oldest, but the compilation also included a song from the Take That era, 'Everything Changes', to justify the fact that the album was celebrating twenty years of Robbie's career. In addition, a 3-CD edition included for the first time a collection of the singer's B-sides, some of which were previously unreleased. Finally, there were two unreleased tracks recorded especially for this compilation: 'Shame' and 'Heart and I'.

'Shame'

Writers: Robbie Williams, Gary Barlow
Duration: 3:59
Released as a single: 27 August 2010
Charts: No. 2 in UK

Robbie Williams and Gary Barlow were angry for many long years after Robbie left Take That in 1995—a break that lasted no less than thirteen years, since the two artists reunited only in 2008. Following this reconciliation, Robbie and Gary considered working together again, and in addition, this reunion allowed the recording of a new Take That album, in full. At the same time, while the singer of 'Angels' was about to release a new compilation—*In and Out of Consciousness*—Robbie and Gary decided to write this track 'Shame', a duet which became the first single resulting from their reunion.

The track was written in just one hour, in February 2010, and it was Trevor Horn—producer of the album *Reality Killed the Video Star* released a few months earlier—who sticks to the song's production. 'Shame' is a country-sounding track, and the music video emphasises that characteristic. Filmed in Los Angeles, just days after the track was recorded, the video features the two men dressed as two modern-day cowboys. The atmosphere is very reminiscent of the movie *Brokeback Mountain*, released five years earlier. In addition to the nod to the theme of cowboys, we find at the end of the clip a very gay scene, which made all fans smile: after exchanges of tender glances, the two men remove their t-shirts and get ready to take the plunge, before finally giving up when they discover the height of the dive they should make.

Humour and tenderness are constantly present in the song. Despite the seriousness of it, Gary indeed slips: 'Oh, and with your poster 30 foot high at the back of Toy-R-Us' and 'I read your mind and tried to call/My tears could fill the Albert hall'. This comeback, fifteen years after their separation, resulted in success: the single ranked No. 2 in the UK Singles Chart.

'Heart and I'

Writers: Robbie Williams, Gary Barlow
Duration: 4:40

'Long Walk Home'

Writers: Martin Page
Duration: 5:09
Extract from the album *In and Out of Consciousness*

'Long Walk Home' is a cover of Martin Page's single (also co-writer of the song 'The Big Good-Bye' that Robbie performed in duet with Ronan Keating in 2020).

Robbie is therefore not the author, but it is one of the most beautiful songs he has interpreted. The poetry of the lyrics can only give you chills, and we can emphasise the elegance of the singer's voice. You are bound to melt!

'Dogs & Birds'

Writers: Robbie Williams
Duration: 4:07
Extract from the album *In and Out of Consciousness*

'Email from a Vampire'

Writers: Robbie Williams, Daniel Spencer Mould, Kelvin Andrews Mould
Duration: 3:21
Extract from the album *In and Out of Consciousness*

This song was probably recorded during the sessions of the album *Reality Killed the Video Star*. Indeed, Robbie's voice is close to the one he has on this album, and here we find Daniel Spencer Mould and Kelvin Andrews Mould, two relatives of the singer, who collaborated in the production of the album.

This song is presented as an email sent by a vampire, played here by Robbie himself. We know his taste for supernatural phenomena, and it is therefore not surprising to see Robbie having fun here on this track.

'Freedom' was the first Robbie Williams single as a solo singer. It is a cover of George Michael's hit 'Freedom', released in 1990.

'No Regrets' was the second single from the second Robbie Williams album, *I've Been Expecting You*. The single includes a B-side, 'Antmusic'. Neil Tennant (The Pet Shop Boys) and Neil Hannon (The Divine Comedy) sing backing vocals on 'No Regrets'.

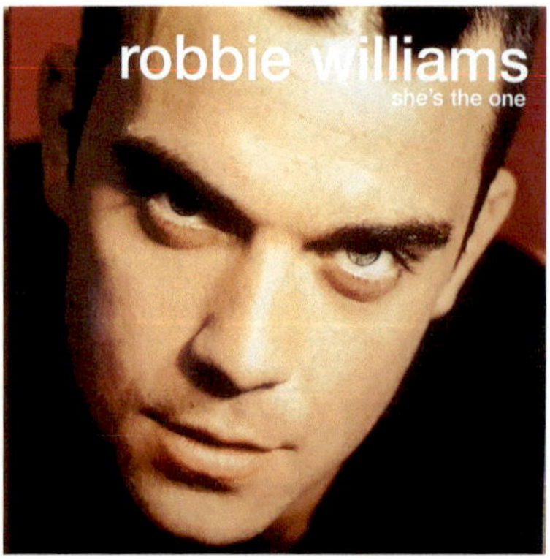

Above: Robbie performed at some music festivals in Europe during the summer of 1999.

Left: 'She's the One' is a cover, but the original song is almost unknown, so it is often considered a Robbie Williams song. The single was No. 1 in the Singles chart.

Above: This is a limited edition release, only available in France. It includes two music videos and a *FIFA 2000* demo.

Below: In 1999, Robbie released the compilation *The Ego Has Landed* in selected areas (USA, Canada, South America, Asia, and Australia). This CD single was released in Mexico.

Above left: In 2002, Robbie lost a trial for using lyrics written by American folk singer Woody Guthrie without permission on the song 'Jesus in a Camper Van'. Consequently, EMI Music was forced to rerelease the compilation *The Ego Has Landed* in order to replace 'Jesus in a Camper Van' with 'Phoenix from the Flames'.

Above right: This is a very rare 3-inch promo CD. It includes only four songs: 'Angels', 'Lazy Days', 'Millennium', and 'Let Me Entertain You'.

Below: This is the promo single released to promote the 'Ask for More Pepsi' campaign. The single includes the song 'United' and a remix ('United – Apollo Four Forty Remix'). The CD also includes a CD-ROM interview.

Above: This concert was planned by French radio station NRJ in order to promote the *Sing When You're Winning* album. It took place in the afternoon (at 5 p.m.).

Below: This promo single was released in France. It contains two songs: 'Suprême' (French version) and 'Often'.

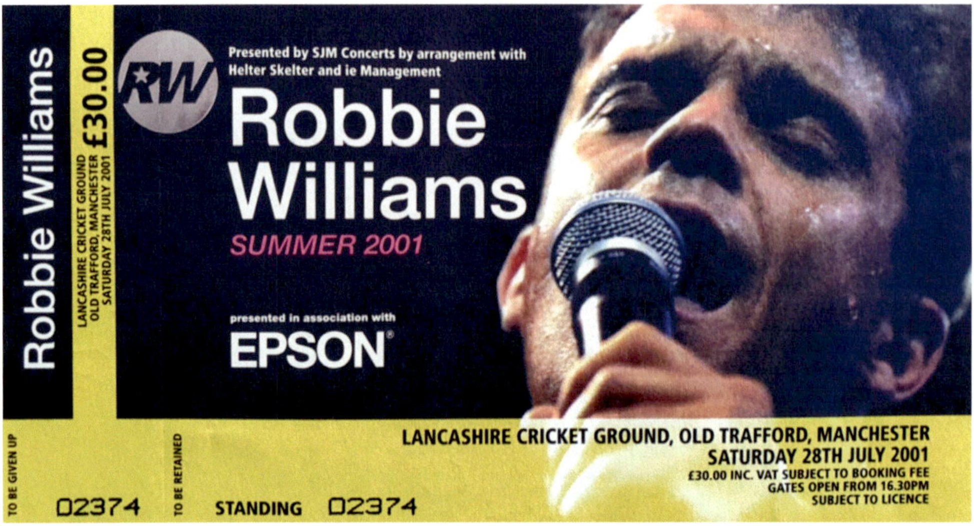

This is a standing ticket, £30 only! Sponsored by Epson, this stadium's tour was named 'Weddings, Barmitzvahs & Stadiums'. It was also simply called 'Summer 2001'.

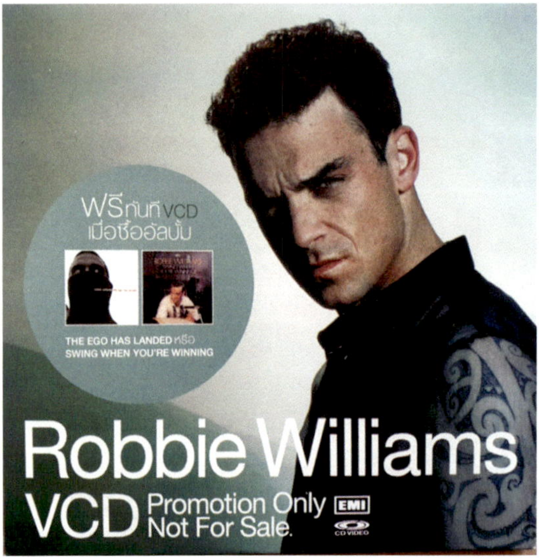

Above left: This is the unique VCD from Robbie Williams's whole career. It contains four karaoke videos.

Above right: The CD album *Sampler* includes only five songs ('Mack the Knife', 'Mr Bojangles', 'Something Stupid', 'One for My Baby', and 'Have You Met Miss Jones'). Inside, a message signed by Robbie says: 'Have you done the X'mas shopping yet? Why not pick *Swing When You're Winning*? You can also make your seasonal donation to my wallet."

Opposite above: This single has never been released. Only a promo CD was released in Mexico.

Opposite below: This is the clean version of *Escapology*. The artwork differs from the commercial release.

Capitol Records
MACK THE KNIFE
ROBBIE WILLIAMS

Robbie Williams
Escapology (clean)

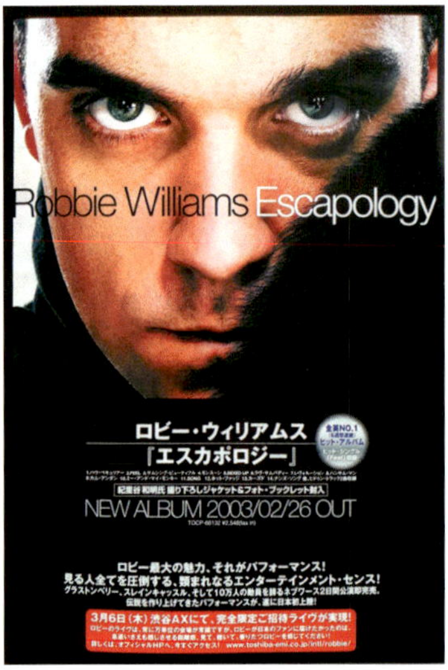

Above: Exclusive artwork for the French release. The CD includes 'Feel' (album version) and 'Nobody Someday' (demo version).

Left: A promo booklet sent to shops to pre-order the Japanese version of *Escapology*.

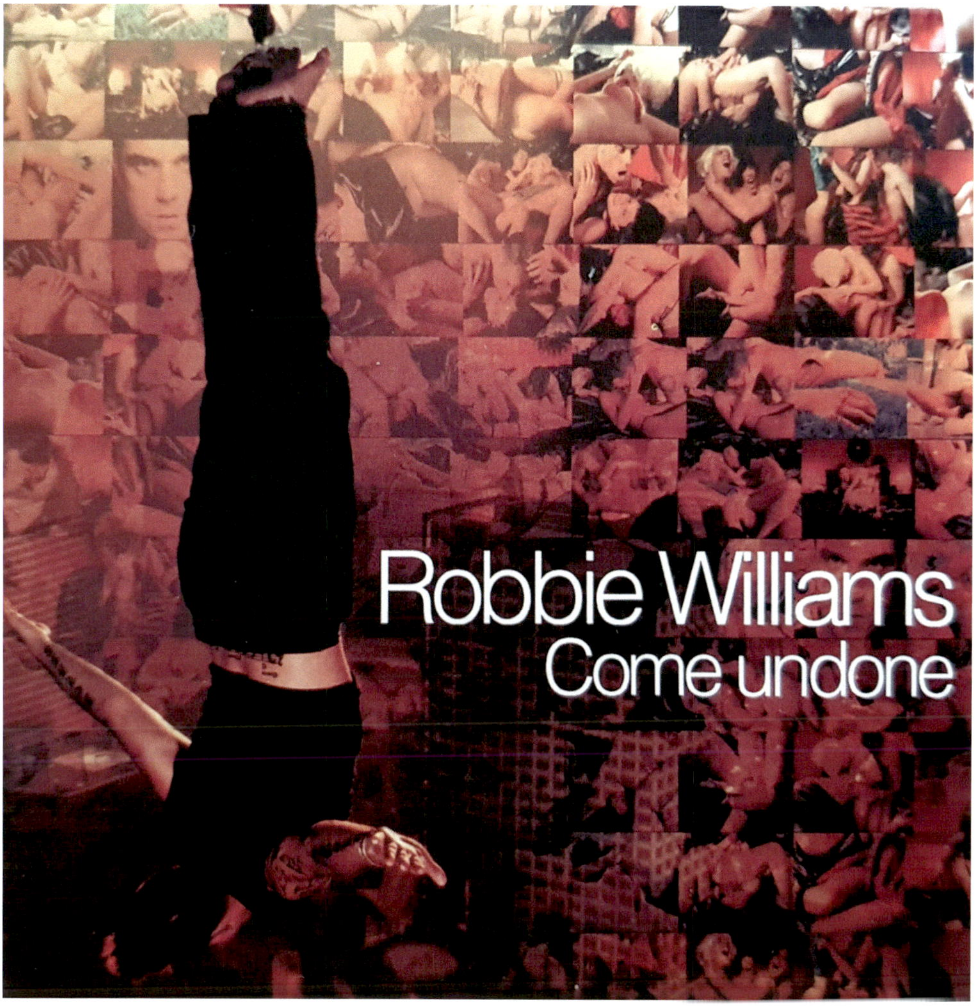

Above: Promo CD for the 'Come Undone' single in Mexico. The front cover mixes the *Escapology* front cover with small pictures from the 'Come Undone' music video. The CD includes a 'Feel' remix (Indigo Sky Remix Feat Lucy), 'Come Undone', and the 'Come Undone' music video.

Right: This CD single was released in France. The front cover picture is taken from the Japanese version of *Escapology*. It includes 'Come Undone', 'One Fine Day', and the 'Come Undone' music video.

Robbie performed a one-off show at Festivalbar in Italy.

Above left: This is a free placement ticket. Sponsored by Smart, this tour was planned to promote *Escapology*.

Above right: When *Greatest Hits* was released, the track list varied depending on the country. Some songs were replaced by others in order to match the popularity of particular songs in some areas. For the Taiwanese edition, the song 'Better Man' was included.

Below: This is the promo version for the *Intensive Care* album. The front cover includes the brand-new Robbie Williams logo that was created exclusively for this album. The logo was used for the album and the Close Encounters Tour the following year.

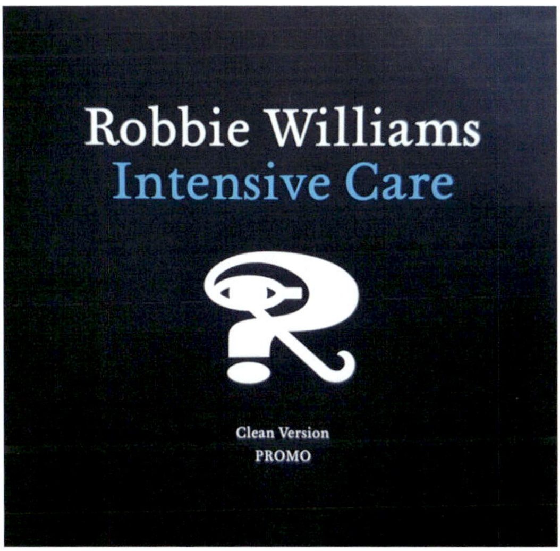

Above left: Robbie at the James Blunt concert at the House of Blues in Los Angeles. Sunset in Los Angeles, California, United States.

Above right: Promo postcard for the release of the compilation *In and Out of Consciousness*.

Below: A concert ticket for the Progress Live Tour in UK with Take That. The artwork is taken from the *Progress* album.

Robbie performing live during the Progress Live Tour in Milan, Italy.

Robbie performing live during the Take the Crown Tour in Milan, Italy, 31 July 2013. (*Photo 185914867 © Fabio Diena Dreamstime.com*)

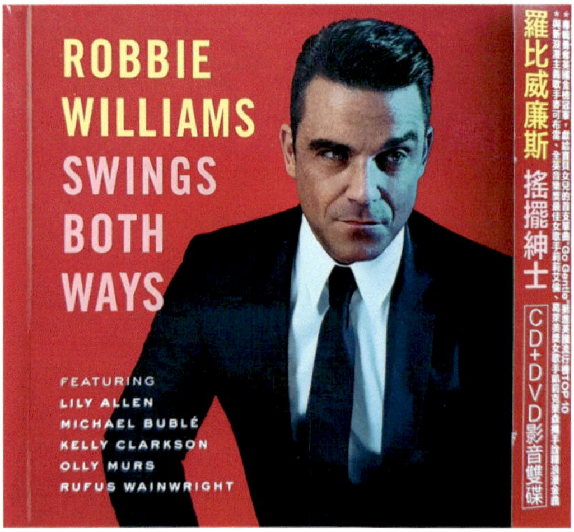

Above left: The deluxe version for *Swings Both Ways*, released in Taiwan.

Above right: The deluxe signed version of *Under the Radar: Volume 1*. This album was released only on the official Robbie Williams website. As a limited edition, only 1,000 copies were pressed.

Above: Robbie performing live during the Take the Crown Tour in Milan, Italy.

Opposite above left: Robbie Williams attends the premiere of *The Sea of Trees* during the sixty-eighth annual Cannes Film Festival, France.

Opposite above right: Robbie Williams performs at Apple Music Festival in London for the launch of his new album, *The Heavy Entertainment Show*.

Opposite below: The Taiwanese edition for *The Heavy Entertainment Show* album.

重度娛樂玩家流行指標
ROBBIE WILLIAMS 羅比威廉斯
THE HEAVY ENTERTAINMENT SHOW 重度娛樂 流行專屬版
☆擁有9張英國金榜冠軍專輯、累積全球7000萬張銷量，英國最強流行天王睽違三年2016強勢壓軸重磅登場
☆驚創音樂史上榮獲17座全英音樂獎最高紀錄
☆收錄〈Party Like A Russian〉搶登比利時榜冠軍，及紅髮艾德創作〈Pretty Woman〉等11首流行玩家專屬單曲
☆內附台灣限定獨家票卡貼紙兩款

Robbie performing at the opening ceremony of the 2018 FIFA World Cup in Russia.

12

Take the Crown

Release date:	5 November 2012
Writers:	Robbie Williams, Tim Metcalfe, Flynn Francis, Jacknife Lee, Gary Barlow, Terje Olsen, Boots Ottestad, Barbara Gruska, Ethan Gruska
Producers:	Jacknife Lee
Studios:	Capitol Studios, The Village Recorders, The Garage, Ocean Studios
Recordings:	September 2011–August 2012
Duration:	43:45
Label:	Island/Universal

After Robbie's Take That parenthesis with the *Progress* album and the Progress Live Tour, fans are a bit lost. Indeed, when he released the previous album, *Reality Killed the Video Star*, everyone expected a tour to accompany it. Instead, he joined his old boy band. Many would say at the time that the Take That interlude had mainly served him to regain his self-confidence on tour, to rebuild his hand.

In 2011, as he was about to go on tour with his former comrades, he revealed to *Esquire* magazine that he was working on new songs with Gary Barlow, and that one of the songs was called 'Candy'. Without knowing it, fans had just learned the name of *Take the Crown*'s debut single, which was released over a year later. This is not the first time this had happened. The singer had already played the song 'Bodies' to his fans in 2008, almost two years before the single was released. Again, everyone was unaware that this song would be the new single.

But back to *Take the Crown*. Originally, Robbie wanted to release a duet album with Gary Barlow, and that is why several songs from the new opus are composed by Gary. But Robbie suddenly changed his mind in 2012 when he met an Australian duo: Tim Metcalfe and Flynn Francis. From then on, the project changed completely, and the album became much more rock than expected.

With this album, Robbie had one goal: to recover his King of Pop crown. For him, it was vital; after crossing the desert between 2007 and 2009, after the discreet success of *Reality Killed the Video Star*, and after taking refuge with Take That, it was time to take back his crown, left aside for a while.

Fortunately, 'Candy' allowed him to come back in force and launch a new tour—his first solo tour for seven years! Even if sales were not what they were (streaming has been there), *Take the Crown* has almost been seen by fans as a new *Escapology*.

'Be a Boy'

Writers: Robbie Williams, Tim Metcalfe, Flynn Francis
Duration: 4:39
Single release date: 11 March 2013
Charts: No. 11 in Belgium

While 'Candy' starts off with one (or more) unexpected trumpets, 'Be a Boy' brings in another unexpected instrument for a Robbie Williams album: the saxophone. While 'Be a Boy' did not make an impression when it was released as a single, as the opening track of the album, it provides a very good overview of the musical style of *Take the Crown* and of the gravelly voice of the singer. In this album, Robbie borrows a more scratchy and more rock voice.

'Gospel'

Writers: Robbie Williams, Tim Metcalfe, Flynn Francis, Jacknife Lee
Duration: 4:25

'Candy'

Writers: Robbie Williams, Gary Barlow, Terje Olsen
Duration: 3:21
Single release date: 11 September 2012
Charts: No. 1 in UK

An immediate hit! When Robbie released 'Candy', he had not had a No. 1 since 2004 with his single 'Radio'. It was eight years before the singer returned to the heights of the UK Singles Chart. What is most amazing about 'Candy' is that Robbie managed to climb to the top of the charts with some very classic instruments (trumpet, violins, and guitar) at a time when everyone swore by the electro, dance, and rap. Robbie himself was arguably surprised to be able to collect a new No. 1, being thirty-eight years old and going in the opposite direction of the current trend.

The introduction to 'Candy' is reminiscent of an alarm clock. From the first notes, the trumpets set the tone, and immediately suggest the start of a story, which can sound like the start of a day. Throughout, the music inspires energy, dynamism, and dance. Another important fact: the lyrics and the tonality exude happiness. The magic of the song also resides in the instrumental contrast: the strong presence of the instruments nevertheless returns an immense feeling of lightness. It is necessary to underline the essential role of the strings, which, by their liveliness, become the true conductor of this piece and dictate to Robbie the rhythm to adopt.

The track is produced extremely well, and every second is likely to suggest excitement, the urge to dance, and a smile. You just have to listen to the instrumental version to be convinced.

'Candy' was such a hit that he managed to impose it with immense ease in the media: the track has been widely used as background music for TV trailers, reports, and teasers. The German channel Prosieben used it to promote its back-to-school programs.

In the track's music video, Robbie shows off the seductive power of a woman, and this is one of the few songs where he does not talk about himself. In the video, Robbie positions himself as an admirer and a guardian angel who protects the young woman portrayed. Filmed in the streets of London, the video calls on many characters, but also many special effects. Note also the irony of the colours chosen. While Robbie is talking about candy ('Candy'), he is the one dressed in pink. This is rather clever, because it subconsciously forms an analogy to viewer that Robbie is a piece of candy!

The young actress, played here by Kaya Scodelario, is instead dressed in blue. The singer does not hesitate to make a fool of himself. His partner, who is unaware of the singer's existence, is well highlighted. So we find the theme of the angel dear to Robbie. While he mentioned the angels in his famous hit of the same name, he himself plays the role of the protective angel.

'Different'

Writers:	Robbie Williams, Gary Barlow, Jacknife Lee
Duration:	4:52
Single release date:	17 December 2012
Charts:	No. 64 in UK

The strings had already convinced us in 'Bodies' and 'Candy', and they are equally convincing here. What stands out here is strength, power. To the strength of the music is added the intensity of the lyrics.

'Different' is aptly named: we cannot really talk about a rock track, though it is not really a ballad either. The song resonates like a cry from the heart, and the production reaches saturation point. No room for silence or for a break. The singer makes desperate promises to his listener: 'This time I'll be different, I promise you/This time I'll be special, you know I will/Just don't leave with me in your eyes'.

After the triumph of 'Candy', 'Different' was Robbie's choice for the album's second single. Despite its intensity and power, the song only reached No. 64 in the charts, one of Robbie's worst. The song undoubtedly suffered from the success of 'Candy', which was still strongly present in the minds of the public. The over-saturated production probably did not help either. Listening to this song on headphones could cause damage to your eardrums.

The music video alternates between black and white footage, in which Robbie plays a criminal, and colour footage, where he plays a conductor, whose musicians are all female. Some images of young women are reminiscent of those in the 'Lovelight' music video.

'Shit on the Radio'

Writers: Robbie Williams, Tim Metcalfe, Flynn Francis, Jacknife Lee
Duration: 2:53

'All That I Want'

Writers: Robbie Williams, Tim Metcalfe, Flynn Francis
Duration: 3:30

'Hunting for You'

Writers: Robbie Williams, Tim Metcalfe, Flynn Francis, Jacknife Lee
Duration: 3:58

'Into the Silence'

Writers: Robbie Williams, Tim Metcalfe, Flynn Francis
Duration: 4:48

While not a single, this track is arguably a fan favourite from the album, alongside 'Candy'. Although 'Into the Silence' is reminiscent of a Depeche Mode hit ('Enjoy the Silence'), the intro is reminiscent of the style of another band from the '80s: U2. The stage is set.

As the seconds go by, the song grows and takes shape. Pushed by upbeat music, Robbie takes the listener by the hand to share his thoughts. This song is a journey that starts with prayer and leads us to silence. In fact, this is not about religious silence, but it is about silence provoked by loneliness, itself triggered by the breakup of love.

The lyrics are unabashedly cruel: 'When karma reaches you I wanna be there to catch that fall/Get down beside you and watch you crawl/How does it feel to be alone?/You happy now?' Faced with the disappointment, the singer reaffirms his resilience in a verse with raucous and unprecedented lyrics: 'I won't fall apart again/You won't break my heart'.

'Hey Wow Yeah Yeah'

Writers: Robbie Williams, Boots Ottestad
Duration: 2:52

The track 'Hey Wow Yeah Yeah' suggests a very festive song and listening to it confirms this. Loud, rock, dynamic, and paired with repetitive lyrics, 'Hey Wow Yeah Yeah' was designed to excite the crowd in concert: 'Clap your hands now/Clap your hands now if you wanna wanna'.

By the way, during the Take the Crown Tour, the track was played as an intro, just before Robbie's came on stage and performed 'Let Me Entertain You'. The song was also used as background music for the 2012 Vauxhall Corsa commercial.

'Not Like the Others'

Writers: Robbie Williams, Tim Metcalfe, Flynn Francis
Duration: 4:15

'Losers'

Writers: Ethan Gruska, Barbara Gruska
Duration: 4:26

'Reverse'

Writers: Robbie Williams, Tim Metcalfe, Flynn Francis
Duration: 3:56

'Eight Letters (Robbie Williams Version)'

Writers: Robbie Williams, Gary Barlow, Mark Owen, Jason Orange, Howard Donald
Duration: 4:40

B-Sides Linked to *Take the Crown*

'On My Own'

Writers: Robbie Williams, Daniel Spencer Mould, Kelvin Andrews Mould
Duration: 3:21
B-side of the single 'Different'

What a pleasure to find here a duet between Robbie and Tom Jones! We had already met this excellent duo in 1998, when the two men sang together on a medley during the Brit Awards, as well as in 1999 on the cover of 'Are You Gonna Go My Way' by Lenny Kravitz.

This time, Robbie and Tom are singing a duet on 'Own My Own', an electro track whose melody is so pleasant and catchy that it is a real pleasure to sing with them, in playback or not! We never tire of hearing the voice of the crooner that is Tom: an inimitable voice, which, accompanied with Robbie's, charms us for sure.

'White Man in Hanoi'

Writers: Robbie Williams, Tim Metcalfe, Flynn Francis
Duration: 3:51
B-side of the single 'Different'

A good rock track, with simple and powerful lyrics. Robbie puts on his sexy, straight, and macho bad boy costume here. A delight for the ears, and listening to the song, we like to imagine what a live performance of the track could have given.

'The Promise'

Writers: Paul Freeman
Duration: 3:47
B-side of the single 'Different'

13

Swings Both Ways

Release date:	18 November 2013
Writers:	Robbie Williams, Guy Chambers, Chris Heath, Richard M. Sherman, Robert B. Sherman, Dino Fekaris, Frederick Perren, Rufus Wainwright, Fabian Andre, Gus Kahn, Wilbur Schwandt, Kelvin Andrews Mould, Scott Ralph, Richard Scott, Danny Spencer Mould, Irving Berlin, Bobby Russell, Cab Calloway, Irving Mills, Clarence Gaskill, Harold Arlen, Yip Harburg, Merle Travis, Gary Barlow
Producers:	Guy Chambers
Studios:	Capitol Studios, Starstruck Studio, Abbey Road Studios, British Grove Studios, Sleeper Sounds, RAK Studio, Sarm Studios, Konk Studios, Angel Recording Studios, Tower of Power Studios
Recordings:	2012–2013
Duration:	56:24
Label:	Island/Universal

This album marks the reconciliation between Robbie and Guy Chambers after ten years of separation. While the two artists had separated in October 2002 when the singer's huge contract was signed with EMI Music, it took until November 2012 to formalise their reunion during concerts given at the O2 in London, during the promotion of *Take the Crown*. Following this, Robbie and Guy Chambers returned to the studio in January 2013 to produce their second swing album: *Swings Both Ways*. This time, the two men were not content with recording covers of great swing classics, and Robbie's mentor deployed his immense talents as a composer to create superb original tracks. The result is stunning: inspired by many cultural references, Guy produced real swing jewels here, some of which could have been very good movie soundtracks. This album provided an opportunity for the singer to perform his first swing tour the following year.

'Shine My Shoes'

Writers:	Robbie Williams, Guy Chambers, Chris Heath
Duration:	3:37
Single release date:	10 December 2013

'Shine My Shoes', a single from the album *Swings Both Ways*, was released twelve years to the day after 'Somethin' Stupid', another swing single from Robbie. This time, however, it was not a cover, but an original track, composed by Robbie, Guy Chambers, and Chris Heath.

This song is a hymn against racism. Robbie took inspiration from Sammy Davis Jr to write it:

> Guy Chambers and I started writing together again after a break of about ten years, and 'Shine My Shoes' came out of the first batch. It's in the spirit of a Sammy Davis Jr. song. In the biopic The Rat Pack there's a dream sequence where Sammy Davis Jr. is dancing against the racists. I'm singing against the haters and the naysayers, giving them my time in the form of a swing song detailing exactly why they should hate me. The smugness will infuriate the haters, and the people who kind of like me will just think that it's sweet.

'Go Gentle'

Writers:	Robbie Williams, Guy Chambers, Chris Heath
Duration:	4:31
Single release date:	10 November 2013
Charts:	No. 10 in UK

This is the lead single from the album *Swings Both Ways*. While the singer was a dad for the first time in September 2012, he decided a year later to record a single dedicated to his daughter, Teddy: 'Go Gentle'.

While this track did not know a dazzling success like his others ('only' No. 10 in the UK Singles Chart), it still touches his audience, charmed by a very pretty song dedicated to his daughter.

On the single's release, the singer shot a music video in the streets of Los Angeles. While a year earlier, he had shot the music video for 'Candy' in the streets of London, this time it was the inhabitants of the City of Angels who were able to enjoy this outdoor shoot.

Here we find the singer dressed in a marine captain's costume, reminiscent of the one he wore in his 'Radio' music video in 2004. The singer walks here on a strange boat, through the streets of Los Angeles, accompanied by a group of musicians dressed as sailors. Dumbfounded, passers-by watch the boat move slowly.

There are some interesting details in the video, such as the presence of the English flag at the front of the boat, or the famous Capitol Records building, symbol of the swing music that Robbie cares so much about.

The video is simple and spontaneous: over the minutes, we understand that the passers-by in the clip are certainly not extras, but members of the public who happened to be there by chance during the filming—some of them are obviously fans of the singer.

'Go Gentle', which is therefore addressed to his daughter, is geared towards the theme of protection. Robbie delivers words that sound like a speech a father might make to his daughter: 'You're gonna meet some strangers, welcome to the zoo/Bitter disappointments, except for one or two'. The singer goes on with a series of tips to warn his daughter of dangers: 'Now when you go dancing with young men down at the disco/ Just keep it simple, you don't have to kiss though'. Above all, he reassures her by telling her that he will always be by her side to help her: 'For all your days and nights (Days and nights)/I'm gonna be there (I'm gonna be there)/I'm gonna be there, yes, I will'.

'I Wanna Be Like You'

Writers: Sherman Brothers
Duration: 3:31

'Swing Supreme'

Writers: Robbie Williams, Guy Chambers, Dino Fekaris, Frederick Perren
Duration: 3:17

Thirteen years after the release of the hit 'Supreme', Robbie offers here a swing version of this song—'Swing Supreme', quite simply—and it is quite successful. The lyrics go very well with the swing style. It reminds me a lot of the one used by George Michael on his very soft cover of the song 'Roxanne' on his album *Songs from the Last Century*—elegance and softness. 'Swing Supreme' was subsequently part of the setlist of the Swings Both Ways Tour in the spring of 2014.

'Swings Both Ways'

Writers: Robbie Williams, Guy Chambers, Rufus Wainwright
Duration: 3:58

This is the song that gave the album the name: *Swings Both Ways*. This is arguably the most sulphurous and funniest track on the album. In English, the expression 'swings both ways' also means 'to be bisexual'. When one knows Robbie's taste for ambiguity and provocation, the choice of this title for both this song and his album is not surprising. In the early 2000s, Robbie often joked about his sexuality, sometimes going so far as to imply that he might be gay or bisexual. If Robbie's heterosexuality is no longer in doubt (he is credited with having numerous relationships, and we know that he is married to Ayda, with whom he had four children), Robbie has himself played with homosexuality both on stage and in interviews. To sum up, one could say that he certainly once considered a same-sex relationship without ever having taken the plunge, and that this slight interest in homosexuality or bisexuality made him extremely tolerant of same-sex couples.

When Robbie recorded the track 'Swings Both Ways', it was therefore not surprising that he did it with openly gay singer Rufus Wainwright. This magical duo is a real treat. Supported by an orchestra, the two men string together funny and provocative innuendos. For example, we are entitled to: 'Face it Robbie/You're a little bit gay' and 'And after I've done her/Well you can do me'.

We also note the instrumental introduction of the song, the music of which inevitably reminds us of the famous musical intros of James Bond. From then on, subconsciously, Robbie and Rufus appear to us as the two special agents of a gay James Bond.

Afraid of no clichés, Robbie decided to be dressed all in pink when the track performed on the Swings Both Ways Live 2014 tour.

'Dream a Little Dream'

Writers: Fabien Andre, Gus Kahn, Wilbur Schwandt
Duration: 3:33
Single release date: 15 December 2013

This is a cover of the song 'Dream a Little Dream of Me', originally performed in 1931 by Ozzie Nelson. 'Dream a Little Dream' is the second single from the album *Swings Both Ways*. Robbie performs this cover with Lily Allen, making this the second time that the two artists have recorded a duet together. We remember their duet on 'Bongo Bong', another cover from the album *Rudebox*.

Although Robbie and Lily also sang 'Dream a Little Dream' on stage during the promotion of the album, the music video does not involve her. In the video, filmed in retro style, Robbie humorously pays homage to Christmas TV shows. While Lily Allen is absent from the video, Guy Chambers is present.

'Soda Pop'

Writers: Robbie Williams, Kelvin Andrews Mould, Scott Ralph, Richard Scott, Danny Spencer Mould
Duration: 3:19

Michael Bublé is arguably the most similar artist to Robbie. While Michael Bublé is more labelled swing singer than Robbie, the two artists are great entertainers, who reveal their talent on stage. Much like the duet with Rufus, the duet with Michael Bublé is not surprising.

The most astonishing here concerns the list of composers of this song. We find here very good friends of Robbie: Kelvin Andrews Mould, Scott Ralph, Richard Scott, and Danny Spencer Mould—all of whom are known to have composed many electro pop songs of the singer, so it is surprising that they end up on a swing-style track. But that is probably why the song nods to pop style by its name: 'Soda Pop'.

We can say that it is rather well found when we know that, in his career, Michael Bublé has succeeded in building a bridge between swing and pop, where Robbie has built a bridge between pop and swing.

'Soda Pop' is therefore defined as a dynamic, light, and sweet song, sealing the perfect marriage between an electro pop icon with swing tunes, with a swing icon with pop accents. To be enjoyed without moderation!

'Snowblind'

Writers: Robbie Williams, Guy Chambers
Duration: 3:19

'Snowblind' is a bit of an oddity to the album. Written and recorded with his friend Guy Chambers in Australia, it has one thing in common with the track 'Blasphemy'; just like this one, the track was composed many years before its release. ('Blasphemy' was written in 2002 during the recording of the *Escapology* album, but it was released only in 2009 on *Reality Killed the Video Star* when 'Snowblind' was recorded back in 2001, but was not realised until 2013—the only track on this album that this is true of).

Regarding 'Snowblind', Robbie says:

> It's from a period in my life when I wanted to be in love, but I knew that I wouldn't be able to do the monogamy thing that was expected of me, and I expected of me too. It caused a lot of relationships to end abruptly....
>
> There was a certain pain attached to that, knowing I wanted to be in love, but also knowing that a twenty-seven-year-old pop star going around the world, meeting girls does what a twenty-seven-year-old pop star I think should do. So it was 'Hey-ho pain, I'll put it in a song and hop into the next bed', but Snowblind is about that period and that pain.

'Puttin' on the Ritz'

Writers: Sherman Brothers
Duration: 3:31

'Little Green Apples'

Writers: Bob Russell
Duration: 3:16

'Minnie the Moocher'

Writers: Cab Calloway, Irving Mills, Clarence Gaskill
Duration: 3:41

'Minnie the Moocher', like 'Dream a Little Dream', dates from 1931. Originally, it is a jazz track, recorded by Cab Calloway and his orchestra, and it has sold over 1 million copies. The song is characterised by the use of scat, a jazz method of improvising by listing a series of meaningless syllables. For example, in 'Minnie the

Moocher', the performer repeats the famous 'Hi De Hi De Hi De Ho' over and over, a method that suits Robbie, who, as we know, loves interacting with the public. As Cab Calloway was doing, Robbie took great pleasure in using this scat, to associate it with another method: that of the call and response. With the call and response, Robbie intones a series of syllables (like 'Hi De Hi De Hi De Ho') and hopes the audience will repeat the same series with the same intonation and energy.

We understand then why Robbie performed this song so often on tour (and not just during the Swings Both Ways Live Tour), because he did not use it only on 'Minnie the Moocher'. The 'Feel' performer has regularly used this method on several tracks. By involving the audience, he makes them adhere to their tastes and style. The result is often the same: the audience, failing in their attempt to emulate Robbie, ends up laughing. Guaranteed atmosphere!

Culturally, the song has been reused numerous times since 1931. In 1932, Calloway recorded a version of the song for a cartoon of the same name, *Minnie the Moocher*. This cartoon featured the famous character Betty Boop and her dog Bimbo. In the cartoon, Betty Boop runs away following an argument with her parents, who wanted to force her to eat. Betty runs away with her dog Bimbo. The two meet in a dark place and hide in a tree. It is then that the ghost of a walrus appears, whose movements were modelled on Calloway's dance. The walrus then begins to sing the track 'Minnie the Moocher' accompanied by many ghosts. After chasing the ghosts, Betty and Bimbo eventually find their way home. Frightened, Betty Boop hides under the sheets, and the letter she had left for her parents is replaced by the words: 'Home Sweet Home'.

Finally, the lyrics of the song would refer to the use of drugs. Indeed, one of the verses can refer to it: 'She messed around with a bloke named Smokey/She loved him though was cokey/He took her down to Chinatown/And he showed her how to kick the gong around'. By 'cokey', the songwriter is referring to someone who takes cocaine, while 'He showed her how to kick the gong around' means 'He showed her how to smoke opium'. Reading the lyrics therefore shows us that the ghosts would be the fruit of the imagination of Betty Boop, who would have smoked too much opium. We then understand that the cartoon is an allegory that tries to prove the dangers of drugs—a story that undoubtedly appealed to Robbie, himself in the grip of his demons.

'If I Only Had a Brain'

Writers: Harold Arlen, Yip Harburg
Duration: 3:52

'No One Likes a Fat Pop Star'

Writers: Robbie Williams, Guy Chambers, Chris Heath
Duration: 2:52

'Where There's Muck'

Writers: Robbie Williams, Guy Chambers
Duration: 4:09

This is one of my favourite songs on the album, probably because its cinematographic aspect appeals to our imagination a lot.

The song begins with the sound of an accordion, accompanied by the sound of seagulls by the sea, slightly tinged with nostalgia. Suddenly, the song evolves towards a more distressing atmosphere, born with the appearance of this sentence: 'There's a sadness in the silent part of me'.

The whole song is written on metaphors related to the theme of the sea. The sea is no longer just a place giving life to romanticism, it also becomes a character whose waves and eddies symbolise rebellion, anger, and bitterness. The singer does not pull any punches, when, helped by the brass, he strikes his blows: 'I'm not asking you/I'm telling you/Kiss my ass/My ass'. Finally, a magnificent energetic finale, carried by the choirs and the orchestra, repeats this verse three times: 'Would've been loved/Should've been loved/Could've been loved'.

This track would have made a great soundtrack without context, and we regret that no music video was made for the occasion.

'16 Tons'

Writers: Merle Travis
Duration: 2:36

'Wedding Bells'

Writers: Robbie Williams, Gary Barlow
Duration: 4:37

B-Sides Linked to *Swings Both Ways*

'You Got Old'

Writers: Robbie Williams, Richard Scott, Scott Ralph, Kelvin Andrews Mould
Duration: 3:45

B-side of the single 'Go Gentle'

Robbie sings a duet here with one of his oldest friend, Jonathan Wilkes. This duet in the form of a dialogue between the two singers evokes, on a swing tune and with humour, the constraints of aging.

14

The Heavy Entertainment Show

Release date:	4 November 2016
Writers:	Robbie Williams, Guy Chambers, Rufus Wainwright, Chris Heath, Serge Gainsbourg, Sergei Prokofiev, Brandon Flowers, Dave Keuning, Mark Stoermer, Ronnie Vannucci Jr, Johnny McDaid, Gary Go, Flynn Francis, Tim Metcalfe, Stuart Price, Jackson Guthy, Kara DioGuardi, Jewel Kilcher, Ed Sheeran, Benjamin Levin, Steve Robson, Mike Curb, Mack David
Producers:	Guy Chambers, Jonny Coffer, Richard Flack, Stuart Price, Steve Robson, Greg Kurstin, Jonny McDaid, Gary Go
Studios:	Sterling Sound
Recordings:	June 2015–June 2016
Duration:	40:03
Label:	Columbia/Sony Music

Since Robbie's return in 2009, every year had been very different for fans of the singer. In six years, the 'Rock DJ' performer had released no less than two pop/rock albums, one album with Take That, one compilation, one swing album, and completed four tours: one tour with Take That, two solo tours, and one swing tour!

Suffice to say that he was not idle, and that the fans were spoiled. But by choosing to diversify more and more projects, Robbie took the risk (or the opportunity) of increasing the delay between each pop album. While between 1997 and 2006, he provided a new pop album every two years on average, this period began to increase from 2009; there was a three-year gap between *Reality Killed the Video Star* and *Take the Crown*, a four-year gap between the latter and *The Heavy Entertainment Show*, and fans are still waiting for its successor.

The Heavy Entertainment Show wants to be the worthy successor of *Take the Crown*. Through the 2012 album, the singer reclaimed his crown of the 'King of Pop', but he claimed his title of 'King of Entertainment' with the 2016 album.

This album undoubtedly has the greatest number of writers and producers of his entire career. Whereas for the previous albums, Robbie often worked with an exclusive writer/producer (Guy Chambers, Stephen Duffy, or Trevor Horn), we find here all the producers who have already worked with the singer in the past, except for Stephen Duffy (it was also rumoured that the two men's partnership had fractured—one more quarrel, one might think) and Mark Ronson (no quarrels here, but there were already enough people on the album).

With so many composers and producers, it is not easy to relate the album to a particular style. Guy Chambers and Rufus Wainwright bring their classic touch, while Australian brothers Tim Metcalfe and Flynn Francis bring a rock collaboration. Finally, Stuart Price (already on *Progress* with Take That) contributes on the album to bring an electro touch.

Two other elements make this album an extraordinary opus: the singer decided to sign a new deal with Sony Music—an unexpected change since he had been with EMI Music since the start of his solo career (joining Universal in 2012 was hardly a choice, given that EMI had just been acquired by Universal). One other element was added to the production of his album: when he had just completed the recording of his new opus, we learned of the death of David Enthoven, the singer's manager since his solo debut. Robbie then decided to include a song in tribute to his manager: 'David's Song'. His second son would later be named after his manager: Beau Benedict Enthoven Williams.

'The Heavy Entertainment Show'

Writers: Robbie Williams, Guy Chambers, Rufus Wainwright, Chris Heath, Serge Gainsbourg
Duration: 3:22

'The Heavy Entertainment Show' is arguably one of Robbie's most dramatised tracks. This song compares the start of a show to that of a boxing match. Robbie has never hidden his love for boxing, and in recent years, he has been seen striking a pose showing his fists like a boxer quite often. The theme of boxing indeed comes up very often in the various promo shoots directed by the best photographers of the time, so it made sense that Robbie would finally dedicate a song to his passion.

After a short, very calm piano intro, the show starts with a bang. The brass resonates to support Robbie's voice, accompanied by frenzied choirs and percussive percussions as we like them. The song features a succession of alternations between calm passages on the piano and grandiose orchestrations.

The song was clearly written to be played in concert. Robbie already had his very famous 'Let Me Entertain You' to open his concerts, but he wanted to give her a little brother. By using the word 'Entertainment', he references the label that the media have attributed to him for years: since 'Let Me Entertain You' and especially since the grandiose concerts such as those of Knebworth in 2003, he is designated as the 'King of Entertainment'.

The song intensifies when the female choirs cry out: 'He would sell his children/For a hit in Belgium/God knows what he's done/For a number one'.

The famous 'Hey, oh, ouh, ah' that come out of the mouths of male choirs at the end of the track are very reminiscent of those of the track 'Bully' released two years earlier on the album *Under the Radar Vol. 1*.

Listening to the lyrics, we recognise here the touch of the composer Robbie: a celebration of the disproportionate ego, combined with a touch of humour that forces a smile. The ego is clearly put forward in this verse: 'Welcome to the Heavy Entertainment Show/The charisma's non-negotiable'. There is also a nod to a very old song by Robbie, 'It's Only Us'. In this last one, he sang: 'We don't want to get a job/We all need a decent rock'. In 'The Heavy Entertainment Show', the rebel Robbie sings this time: 'Why not leave your job and come on tour with us?' Moreover, the two songs also have in common the fact that their duration is very short. Indeed, both last exactly 3:22—a duration that must surely stick to Robbie for rock tracks, since 'Bully', mentioned above, lasts 3:21. The smile arises when the singer announces cynically: 'Even you will leave here with a t-shirt and a program/Got a house in LA, I'm still paying for it'. Self-mockery is taken to a climax, when the choirs cry out: 'He would sell his children/For a hit in Belgium/God knows what he's done/For a number one'.

However, the song 'The Heavy Entertainment Show' is arguably one of the greatest errors of the singer's career. While the song is particularly good, and while the singer will shoot a great music video for it, the song has never been released as a single. When the album's promo kicked off in September 2016, fans were only getting snippets of the music video, and they had to wait until the spring of 2017 to see the video in its entirety. Robbie instead preferred to release the track 'Party Like a Russian' as the first single—a rather confusing choice!

'Party Like a Russian'

Writers:	Robbie Williams, Guy Chambers, Sergei Prokofiev, Chris Heath
Duration:	3:02
Single release date:	30 September 2016
Charts:	No. 68 in UK

After the immense success of 'Candy' in 2012—a song which managed to be No. 1 in the UK Singles Chart with a mostly classical instrumentation—Robbie undoubtedly thought that he could repeat the feat, with his new single, 'Party Like a Russian'. Indeed, we find here a certain desire to go against the grain: the song calls for an equally very classical orchestration, and even goes so far as to borrow and sample the very famous piece 'Montagues and Capulets' (also called 'Dance of the Knights') by Russian composer Sergei Prokofiev.

As we know, Robbie is used to samples, especially when working with Guy Chambers. We remember the famous samples used for 'Millennium', 'Rock DJ', and 'Supreme'. But this time around, the bet failed: 'Party Like a Russian' ranked only No. 68 in UK sales.

It must be said that unlike 'Candy', which had been No. 1, 'Party Like a Russian' does not bring joy, excitement, or celebration. We tend to think that by recording 'Party Like a Russian', Robbie wanted to create a work of art rather than a new hit. The song samples a piece of Russian classical music to talk about a certain Russian way of life. Moreover, behind the purely artistic aspect of the song lies a new controversy, and 'Party Like a Russian' was one of the singer's most controversial singles.

Even today, it is very difficult to understand what the singer's intentions were when he wanted to release this single. To try to understand it, we have to go back to the context. When the song premiered in 2016, Robbie enjoyed a rather positive image in Russia; he had already given many concerts there, and the most indiscreet fans had noticed that their idol had given several private concerts for Russian billionaires since 2012.

Inspired by the Russian oligarchy, one can imagine that Robbie wanted to devote a song to this theme. But where the trouble set in was when the media found out about the song's lyrics and music video. Although the singer denies having wanted to criticise Russia with this track, the Russian media did not hear it in the same way, and then decided to boycott this musical affront outright. Some local media went so far as to call Robbie a has-been. It must be said that it does not pull any punches, especially from a video point of view.

The song starts deftly with male and military choirs uttering 'Hey, hey!' These echo the very manly 'Hey, oh, ouh, ah' from 'The Heavy Entertainment Show'. The song features the famous sample inspired by 'Dance of the Knights' which loops throughout the song. We then dive completely into Russia, when the military choirs come into play. But the song takes all its power in the music video which is full of details.

First, we notice the young girl whose tongue is golden. We can see two meanings: the golden colour on the tongue can symbolise the sin of gluttony (gluttony for luxury or money), but also disgust (the same young girl sticks her tongue out a second time in the video, with an air of disgust).

Moreover, we can see a link with the music video of 'The Heavy Entertainment Show'. In it, golden liquid escapes from Robbie's nose—perhaps to show another cardinal sin, anger? Another provocative moment is when Robbie wipes his nose, as if he had just taken drugs.

A more political detail this time: on the long table in the dining room, at which Robbie is seated, there is a newspaper showing a flag of the European Union. This is almost certainly a snub to Vladimir Putin. In the same way, one wonders if Robbie is criticising Russian power—power known to discriminate against homosexuality; in fact, two female characters wear makeup representing a black heart. These two young women also have a sad expression on their faces. One can imagine that these two hearts are 'in mourning' because they know that homosexuality is not really accepted in Russia.

But Robbie seems to give an optimistic connotation to the video, with a passage where the young women seem to revolt and run. Dressed in wedding dresses, they are celebrating in the garden, with an ice cream in their hands. This gives a very strong image as the young women are reminiscent of statues of Liberty in motion (the ice cream representing the flame of the statue of Liberty, an American icon).

Finally, it is unknown exactly who the final middle finger at the end of the music video is aimed at. We know that a year and a half later, the singer repeated the gesture during the opening ceremony of the World Cup which took place in Russia, so we can only assume.

'Mixed Signals'

Writers:	Brandon Flowers, Dave Keuning, Mark Stoermer, Ronnie Vannucci Jr
Duration:	3:58
Single release date:	28 February 2017

The track 'Mixed Signals' was written by The Killers and produced by Stuart Price. The band gave this song to Robbie. 'Mixed Signals' benefits from very modern sounds, and the music video is in the same vein. We quickly get attached to this track whose contours are very rock, and whose lyrics are very down to earth: 'I tried your number at nine but to no avail/Tried again at eleven, got sent straight to voicemail/You said you needed a calm, quiet night alone'.

In the video, the singer, locked in a hotel room, tries unsuccessfully to call his partner, who is in lovely company. For this adultery-themed clip, three alternate endings were shot, including one with his wife Ayda Field and one with Gary Barlow.

'Love My Life'

Writers:	Robbie Williams, Johnny McDaid, Gary Go
Duration:	3:28
Single release date:	20 November 2016
Charts:	No. 22 in UK

Robbie has mostly accustomed us to melancholy walks, songs featuring his demons, or quite rhythmic electro/rock songs. Here he breaks tradition, this time with one of the most optimistic tracks in his catalogue. 'Love My Life' is optimistic to its core. It is the opposite of the track 'Strong' in which the singer confessed his weaknesses. In 'Love My Life', he affirms his strengths and his *joie de vivre* without any ambiguity: 'I love my life/I am powerful/I am beautiful/I am free'.

Originally, I did not like this song, the lyrics of which might sound a bit cutesy or too simplistic. But after listening several times, we let ourselves be seduced by his positive lyricism. At a time when we are constantly confronted with our doubts, fears, and dark thoughts, hearing such a song is invigorating. Finally, it should be noted that the singer alludes to his hit 'Angels' in this verse: 'I started to question the angels/And the answer they gave was you'.

'Motherfucker'

Writers: Robbie Williams, Tim Metcalfe, Flynn Francis, Chris Heath
Duration: 4:17

'Bruce Lee'

Writers: Robbie Williams, Stuart Price
Duration: 4:13

'Sensitive'

Writers: Robbie Williams, Stuart Price, Jackson Guthy
Duration: 3:16

'David's Song'

Writers: Robbie Williams, Guy Chambers, Kara Dioguardi, Jewel
Duration: 4:14

This song is dedicated to David Enthoven, Robbie's former manager, who died on 11 August 2016, a few months before the album was released. David accompanied Robbie during the first twenty years of his solo career, a considerable amount of time. Later, in 2020, Robbie chose to name his fourth child Beau Benedict Enthoven Williams—suffice to say that David really marked the life of the singer.

'Pretty Woman'

Writers: Robbie Williams, Ed Sheeran, Benjamin Levin, Chris Sclafani, Steve Robson
Duration: 2:56

'Hotel Crazy'

Writers: Robbie Williams, Guy Chambers, Rufus Wainwright
Duration: 4:25

'Sensational'

Writers: Robbie Williams, Guy Chambers, Rufus Wainwright, Chris Heath, Mike Curb, Mack David
Duration: 3:48

'Sensational' was first a live track before being a studio song; indeed, it is the song that closed the concerts of the Swings Both Ways Live Tour. Robbie decided to include it on this album. This track has not gone unnoticed by fans: not only is the song rather catchy and pleasant to listen to, but, in addition, the lyrics are particularly provocative. With his trademark cheeky air, Robbie asks his fans to leave the room: 'And I wish that you could always stay/Now go away'. Fans also enjoyed this other provocation: 'You've been affectionate/You dirty bunch of sluts'.

'When You Know'

Writers: Robbie Williams, Guy Chambers, Jimmy Carr
Duration: 4:21

'Time On Earth'

Writers: Robbie Williams, Guy Chambers, Chris Heath
Duration: 4:51

'I Don't Want to Hurt You'

Writers: Robbie Williams, Guy Chambers, John Grant
Duration: 4:19

'Best Intentions'

Writers: Robbie Williams, Guy Chambers, Chris Heath
Duration: 3:44

'Marry Me'

Writers: Robbie Williams, Karl Brail, Benjamin Roy Castle
Duration: 3:54

15

The Christmas Present

Release date:	22 November 2019
Writers:	Robbie Williams, Guy Chambers, Benjamin Roy Castle, Brahim Fouradi, Carlos Vrolijk, Danny Spencer Mould, Edwin Serrano, Ellie Greenwich, Felix Bernard, Flynn Francis, Greg Lake, Jeff Barry, Jim Lea, Joan Javits, John Garrison, Jule Styne, Karl Brazil, Kelvin Andrews Mould, Konrad Olsen, Martin Terefe, Mel Tormé, Memru Renjaan, Noddy Holder, Owen Parker, Peter Sinfield, Phil Spector, Philip Springer, Philipp Steinken Richard B. Smith, Richard Scott, Robert Wells, Sam Sure, Sammy Cahn, Scott Ralph, Sylvia Moy, Tim Metcalfe, Tom Longworth, Tony Springer, William 'Mickey' Stevenson
Producers:	Robbie Williams, Guy Chambers, Soul Mekanik, Daft Dog, Richard Flack
Studios:	Sleeper Sounds, Angel Recording Studios, RAK Studio, Sylvia Young Studio, Kensaltown Studios, Sarm West Coast, Green Nova Studios, LMA Studio, Rocklands, Burslem School of Art, Realstrings, Wonk, The Warehouse Studio
Recordings:	June 2019–September 2019
Duration:	92:06
Label:	Columbia/Sony Music

After the *Swing When You're Winning* and *Swings Both Ways* albums, Robbie's crooning skills are well established. However, Robbie does not like to repeat himself. While the first swing album was mostly made up of covers, and the second included many original tracks, the singer this time opted for a Christmas-themed swing album. The recording of *The Christmas Present* was also prompted in part by insistent fan requests made on the official app. But is it really a swing album? While most of the album revolves around this style, some songs have more modern sounds, quite far from swing. This is the case for example of the songs 'Bad Sharon' and 'Time for Change', which though not swing in style are at the very least Christmas themed.

This is the singer's first double album, and therefore the longest: more than ninety-two minutes of music, with twenty-nine tracks in total if we count the bonus tracks from the deluxe edition and the unreleased track 'Can't Stop Christmas' released one year later.

'Winter Wonderland'

Writers: Richard Smith, Felix Bernard
Duration: 2:20

'Merry Xmas Everybody'

Writers: Slade
Duration: 3:48

'Let It Snow! Let It Snow!'

Writers: Sammy Cahn, Jule Styne
Duration: 1:58

'The Christmas Song (Chestnuts roasting on an open fire)'

Writers: Robert Wells, Melvin H. Mel Torme
Duration: 3:13

'Coco's Christmas Lullaby'

Writers: Robbie Williams, Kelvin Andrews Mould, Richard Scott, Daniel Spencer Mould
Duration: 2:56

'Rudolph'

Writers: Robbie Williams, Kelvin Andrews Mould, Richard Scott, Daniel Spencer Mould, Robert Mellin, Gian Piero Reverberi
Duration: 3:37

'Yeah! It's Christmas'

Writers: Robbie Williams, Kelvin Andrews Mould, Scott Ralph, Richard Scott
Duration: 2:49

'It's a Wonderful Life'

Writers: Robbie Williams, Kelvin Andrews Mould, Richard Scott, Daniel Spencer Mould
Duration: 2:52

'Let's Not Go Shopping'

Writers: Robbie Williams, Kelvin Andrews Mould, Richard Scott, Daniel Spencer Mould
Duration: 3:10

You could describe 'Let's Not Go Shopping' as an anti-Christmas song! While the holiday season is often synonymous with shopping to please those you love, Robbie suggests here not to shop!

Recorded with full orchestra, like many tracks from *The Christmas Present*, 'Let's Not Go Shopping' has a distinctly swing sound, and it is perfectly suited for the Christmas theme.

The song opens with male backing vocals; this is unusual as Robbie most often uses female backing vocals to accompany his tracks, but it is yet another way to stand out. 'Let's Not Go Shopping' is a pretty clever track, reminding listeners that the essence of Christmas is in the love and magic of the holidays, rather than in shopping.

'Santa Baby'

Writers: Joan Javits, Philip Springer, Tony Springer
Duration: 3:28

'Best Christmas Ever'

Writers: Robbie Williams, Guy Chambers
Duration: 3:46

'One Last Christmas'

Writers: Robbie Williams, Flynn Francis, Konrad Olsen
Duration: 3:34

'Coco's Christmas Lullaby Reprise'

Writers: Robbie Williams, Kelvin Andrews Mould, Richard Scott, Daniel Spencer Mould
Duration: 1:18

'Time for Change'

Writers: Robbie Williams, Guy Chambers, Karl Brazil, Tom Longworth
Duration: 3:30
Single release date: 22 November 2019

You only have to watch the 'Time for Change' music video to be convinced that it is a bit of a sequel to 'Somethin 'Stupid', eighteen years later. Why? Quite simply because both tracks and both videos have many similarities. In both videos, the scene takes place at Christmas, in a house, and in both cases, the singer is in a relationship: If Nicole Kidman plays the role of Robbie's wife in 'Somethin 'Stupid', Ayda Field plays the role in 'Time for Change'.

This is Ayda's third appearance in a singer's music video: the young woman was already featured in the 'Bodies' music video in 2009, then in the 'Mixed Signals' video in 2016. Another similarity: 'Somethin' Stupid' and 'Time for Change' both came out at Christmas (10 December 2001 and 22 November 2019, respectively).

On the other hand, 'Time for Change' is intended to be more family-friendly; while 'Somethin 'Stupid' featured a couple and a few friends, 'Time for Change' involves children and dogs to complete the family.

This song is a reflection on the passage of time. Robbie encourages us to use the holidays to spend time with family, because he knows that time flies quickly, cruelly quickly: 'But while we're all still here on Earth/Sing about love and forget about loss/And shout for whatever you're worth'.

'Idlewild'

Writers: Robbie Williams, Karl Brazil, Tim Metcalfe
Duration: 4:09

'Darkest Night'

Writers: Robbie Williams, Karl Brazil, Owen Parker
Duration: 3:20

'Fairytales'

Writers: Robbie Williams, Karl Brazil, John Garrison, Martin Terefe
Duration: 3:34

'Christmas (Baby please come home)'

Writers: Elie Greenwich, Jeff Barry, Phil Spector
Duration: 2:42

'Bad Sharon'

Writers: Robbie Williams, Karl Brazil, Benjamin Roy Castle
Duration: 3:40

'Bad Sharon' is arguably the most unexpected and surprising song on *The Christmas Present* album. It is unexpected because Robbie sings here in duet with a boxing champion, Tyson Fury. For the record, the singer met him a few months before the duet recording, behind the scenes of a match he had attended. 'Bad Sharon' remains the boxer's only musical adventure to this day. It is surprising because even if the song evokes the end of year holiday period ('Can't believe it's Christmas/Can't believe it's Christmas again'), and even if the atmosphere is rather festive, the lyrics guide us more towards a more vulgar theme, which describes an office party that goes wrong: 'Grab Bad Sharon from the office/Nick the champagne, let's get off it/Just in time for Auld Lang Syne'.

Funnily enough, the famous website vice.com described 'Bad Sharon' as the Christmas song of the century, suggesting times really have really changed.

'Happy Birthday Jesus Christ'

Writers: Robbie Williams, Flynn Francis, Konrad Olsen, Philipp Steinke
Duration: 3:16

'New Year's Day'

Writers: Robbie Williams, Karl Brazil, Benjamin Roy Castle
Duration: 3:42

'Snowflakes'

Writers: Robbie Williams, Flynn Francis, Konrad Olsen, Philipp Steinke
Duration: 3:42

'Home'

Writers: Robbie Williams, Owen Parker, Sam Sure, Karl Brazil
Duration: 4:11

It is my favourite song on *The Christmas Present* album, and arguably one of the best songs of Robbie's career. Listening to this track, and these words, one can easily imagine Robbie singing this track to his children on Christmas Eve. 'Home' resonates like a soft lullaby, tender and comforting. The musical intro of the title envelops us like a warm blanket, before the singer's voice arrives.

As in many Robbie songs, we find here the theme of passing time: 'Tell me where the autumn went, I missed it/Spring and summer flew by in an instant'. This song is overflowing with so much love and generosity that it can only make you crack, and sometimes make you cry. Each new hearing of this track capsizes me, because it arouses emotion, nostalgia, and comfort.

As a good, loving father, Robbie promises the children he loves: 'I told you I'm never too far away/And if you need me then I'm on my way/Believe me when I tell you that I wanna stay/And we're all together now'.

'Home' truly represents the perfect song that a father can sing to his children, or that a child can dream of hearing. Without a doubt, the pearl of *The Christmas Present* album.

'Soul Transmission'

Writers: Robbie Williams, Kelvin Andrews Mould, Richard Scott, Daniel Spencer Mould
Duration: 4:14

This track first appeared in 2012, on the EP *Different*, the second single from *Take the Crown*. The presence of this track on the album *The Christmas Present* is quite unexpected. Besides being unreleased, this track has no swing sound like most of the other songs on the album. Indeed, we are faced with electro sounds. The track is produced by Soul Mekanik and Daft Dog, two producers on *Rudebox*.

We can explain the presence of this track probably because of the lyrics, since the song contains this line in particular: 'I said it feels like being/Alone on Christmas day'. But the images of the music video make us understand that Robbie is highlighting his marriage with Ayda (they got married in 2010).

'I Believe in Father Christmas'

Writers: Greg Lake, Pete Sinfield, Sergueï Prokofiev
Duration: 3:11

'Not Christmas'

Writers: Robbie Williams, Flynn Francis, Tim Metcalfe
Duration: 3:26

'Merry Christmas'

Writers: Robbie Williams, Brahim Fouradi, Edwin Serrano, Memru Renjaan, Carlos Vrolijk
Duration: 2:43

'It Takes Two'

Writers: Sylvia Moy, William Stevenson
Duration: 3:53

'Can't Stop Christmas'

Writers: Robbie Williams, Karl Brazil, Owen Parker, Chris Heath, Benjamin Roy Castle
Duration: 3:23
Single release date: 20 November 2020

This song was released in the specific context of the COVID-19 pandemic. While the album *The Christmas Present* was released just before the pandemic, at the end of 2019, Robbie considered releasing a reissue of his album a year later, at the end of 2020. Originally, he intended to release a reissue that included seven unreleased tracks (the idea was to remove seven tracks from the original edition and replace them with seven new ones). This project was eventually scrapped (presumably due to the pandemic), and, instead, only one track was recorded: 'Can't Stop Christmas'.

The song's message is clear: despite the various lockdowns and restrictions linked to the crisis, Christmas cannot be cancelled. It was Ayda who suggested Robbie record this title, and the result is quite successful. The singer first makes a realistic observation: 'Oh what a miserable year/But what a time to be alive/Sadly some friends disappeared'. And further, faced with the sad reality, Robbie gives us his comforting: 'Nothing's gonna stop Christmas/No chance'.

But of this song, we especially remember the music video. As is often the case with Robbie, we are treated to a lot of his playful attitude here. It features Robbie disguised as Boris Johnson, as well as a woman resembling former Prime Minister Theresa May.

'Can't Stop Christmas' is also the first single from Robbie to have known no physical support: the track has never been released as a physical single, and no physical reissue of the album has been made, meaning this song is not available on any CD or vinyl.

16

XXV

Release date:	9 September 2022
Producers:	Guy Chambers, Jules Buckley, Richard Flack
Studios:	Sleeper Sounds, RAK Studio, Air-Edel Studios, Empire Studio, Snap! Studio, Rosewood Music, Klabang Studio, 301 Studios, Green Nova Studios, Angel Recording Studios, Emil Berliner Studios
Duration:	76:04
Label:	Columbia/Sony Music

Just before the arrival of COVID-19, Robbie's management had indicated that a 'best of' celebrating Robbie's twenty-five-year solo career was to be released at the end of 2020, before a huge tour on the same theme in 2021. But obviously, the pandemic halted all of his projects.

We had to wait until September 2022 to see this project come forth. Its name: *XXV*. In this new compilation (sometimes considered an album), Robbie re-recorded his greatest hits, in a swing version, accompanied by a Dutch symphony orchestra, the Metropole Orkest. Produced by Guy Chambers, Jules Buckley, and Richard Flack, *XXV* includes no less than twenty-nine songs on its deluxe version.

We note the excellent new version of 'No Regrets', which is built on a sample of the famous James Bond theme song 'Diamonds Are Forever', interpreted originally by Shirley Bassey. This choice is explained quite simply: Guy Chambers undoubtedly wanted to give a little brother to the single 'Millennium' (which contained another sample of a James Bond film, *You Only Live Twice*, whose theme song had been interpreted at the time by another grande dame, Nancy Sinatra). The two singles were part of the album *I've Been Expecting You*, whose artwork was inspired by the British secret agent—the plan came full circle. Besides this nod, we note the new version of the title 'Nobody Someday'. This title was originally a simple B-side, and we are surprised by its presence here.

XXV also includes an amazing version of 'Better Man'. While its original version directed us towards a positive melody, this new version on the contrary borrows a much more melancholy and sad voice. But when we know that the biopic whose title is named after the song is scheduled for November 2023, we guess that the meaning of this version will gain full clarity once inserted into the film.

Another surprise: the Beethoven AI version of his greatest hit 'Angels'. With the help of an exclusive partnership with German operator Deutsche Telekom, Robbie offers here a version that has been designed by artificial intelligence. And why Beethoven? Quite simply because this song was to be released in 2020, on the 250th anniversary of Beethoven's birth. 'Angels (Beethoven AI)' is without doubt one of Robbie's finest songs. The last part of the track actually takes us in a solemn, dramatic, and elegant approach, driven by a set of violins that particularly appeals to our emotion. A jewel.

The *XXV* album also includes five unreleased tracks.

'Lost'

Writers: Robbie Williams, Oli Swan, Guy Chambers, Chris Heath
Duration: 3:38

Despite a brand-new music video shot in Martigues, in the south of France, the track did not convince fans, and Robbie himself tends not to qualify it as a hit, especially since the melody is a bit too similar to another single, 'Love My Life', which was much more successful.

'More Than This'

Writers: Robbie Williams, Karl Brazil, Owen Parker
Duration: 4:10

'Disco Symphony'

Writers: Robbie Williams, Guy Chambers, Jimmy Carr
Duration: 3:51

We already knew this track which was originally part of the soundtrack of the musical *The Boy in the Dress*. Here is a version interpreted by Robbie for the first time.

'Home Thoughts from Abroad'

Writers: Robbie Williams, Guy Chambers
Duration: 3:22

Like the previous track, it is also a song from a movie soundtrack, on which Robbie finally puts his voice. The film in question is *Military Wives*, released in 2019.

'The World and Her Mother'

Writers: Robbie Williams, Karl Brazil, Owen Parker
Duration: 4:12

17

Under the Radar

Over the years, Robbie has recorded many tracks. While many songs made their way onto the albums and singles he released, many others did not, either because they were too weak compared to the others or because their style did not match the style of the album. But Robbie, having accumulated a significant number of songs put aside, did not like the thought that these songs would remain hidden forever. Thus came the idea of releasing a series of albums of these famous songs. The singer called this series *Under the Radar*. To date, three volumes have been released: the first was released in December 2014, the second in November 2017, and the third in February 2019. It is not known if this series will see other volumes. At the start of the 2017 tour, Robbie indicated that he wanted to release a total of five volumes. However, fans agree that Volume 3 is weaker than the previous two, and as a result, it is not clear that Volumes 4 and 5 will ever come out.

Besides the fact that these albums bring together songs that were put aside in the past, they have another special feature: they were put on sale exclusively on the official website. No release in the traditional trade took place. Finally, a third peculiarity should be noted: for each of the three volumes, Robbie must have spent hours signing by hand the deluxe editions that the fans had ordered.

Volume 1

'Bully'

Writers: Robbie Williams, Tim Metcalfe, Flynn Francis
Duration: 3:21

This song is undoubtedly an exception in the concept of the *Under the Radar* albums. While these albums are supposed to gather tracks from the past, 'Bully' was written only a few months before the release of the first volume of the series. Indeed, the song was composed in September 2014 in Australia, during the Swings Both Ways Live Tour, just three months before the album's release. In fact, 'Bully' was recorded to serve as the soundtrack for Café Royal's new advertising campaign, of which Robbie was their new ambassador. The deal with the Swiss coffee brand was scheduled for four years.

In the Café Royal ad campaign, Robbie takes on the role of a secret agent, and similar to the famous James Bond, he is surrounded by attractive young women and wearing a suit with bowtie. The only difference, no doubt, is a pronounced taste for self-mockery.

Robbie explains that with this song he wanted to express, with exaggeration, what he would like to do to certain people he does not like, and listening to the track, you can tell it is that feeling that stands out. Here, the singer opts for a serious and threatening tone. Refinement and violence coexist in this incisive song. A very manly 'Uuh ah!!' alternating with the clicks of loaded guns and gunshots echoed throughout 'Bully'. It is arguably Robbie's most violent song, not just for his music, but also for his lyrics: 'I simply don't care/if you hate me or love me/pass me the pistol/shot the bullet!!'

Even though 'Bully' was not released as a single, the track is almost considered as such, as it is the first track from *Under the Radar: Volume 1* that was unveiled, and the Café Royal advertisement relying on him, it offered up some good media exposure. In fact, it could almost be compared to the 'United' song, released in 2000, which was also used to launch an advertising campaign for another drink: Pepsi.

'Raver'
Writers: Robbie Williams, Tim Metcalfe, Flynn Francis
Duration: 3:56

'H.E.S'
Writers: Robbie Williams, Tim Metcalfe, Flynn Francis
Duration: 4:05

'The Edge'
Writers: Robbie Williams, Guy Chambers, Chris Heath
Duration: 4:08

'All Climb On'
Writers: Robbie Williams, Guy Chambers
Duration: 4:35

'Surrender'
Writers: Robbie Williams, Tim Metcalfe, Flynn Francis
Duration: 4:06

'Love Is You'
Writers: Robbie Williams, Jerry Meehan
Duration: 3:44

'The Cure'

Writers: Robbie Williams, Guy Chambers, Chris Heath
Duration: 4:11

'The Pilot'

Writers: Robbie Williams, Guy Chambers, Justin Nozuka, Chris Heath
Duration: 3:50

Once again, we can guess here the influence of George Michael listening to 'The Pilot'. Combining both electro music, sometimes effeminate vocals, and male choirs, 'The Pilot' could very well have been performed by the former member of Wham! Even the choice of words makes you think of George Michael. In the lyrics, we can indeed hear: 'You can't be/Just lying in your bed/Lying there alone/It's not right babe'.

The beat also suggests George's style, when Robbie speeds up to sing: 'We're unbeatable/Yes, your heart beats the rhythm inside of my chest'. In fact, it is to be believed that Robbie really made it his mission to emulate the style of George Michael when he recorded this song. All the ingredients are there: choice of rhythm, choice of words, sound, and voice. It feels like being on the *Patience* album.

'The Brits'

Writers: Robbie Williams, Guy Chambers
Duration: 4:55

This song has a story. As a reminder, Robbie is the artist with the most Brit Awards—eighteen in total! Despite this absolute record, the singer did not hesitate to express his cynicism, through this song. While he came to sing his hit 'Candy' at the Brit Awards on 20 February 2013, Robbie released a song called 'The Brits 2013' a few days later to criticise the ceremony he just attended! It is this track, now titled 'The Brits', that can be found on the album *Under the Radar: Volume 1*.

In February 2013, Robbie released this new song, which can be downloaded for free on the official website, where he warns: 'Here's a gift from me and guy.... We wrote it on Saturday, recorded it on Sunday.... If you have kids in the room, don't play it'. The song starts with an excerpt from an interview with Robbie, an interview quickly distorted into 'Bla bla bla, bla bla bla', before moving on to a rap, whose style is very close to the song 'The 90s' from the album *Rudebox*.

Here we find the provocative Robbie listing a series of scathing phrases of which only he has the secret. Among his invectives, we find in particular this verse: 'Coke in the bogs till seven in the morning/Look the wrong way and we end up brawling/When I had a bit of beef with you know who/And I fucked a few female stars or two'.

While the media pointed out that this song appeared to be an attack made at the Brit Awards ceremony, we cannot really agree with them. The song deals more with the excesses of stardom than the ceremony itself. Moreover, the organisers of the Brit Awards never held it against him, since in 2016, they awarded Robbie his eighteenth Brit Award (an Icon Award), and in 2017, they again invited the singer to perform a medley at that year's ceremony.

'National Treasure'

Writers: Robbie Williams, Guy Chambers, Chris Heath
Duration: 4:26

Watch out, another song that has become a fan favourite not just because it is particularly brilliant, but also because its performance has been the subject of much discussion among fans. Indeed, many fans have wondered who the song is about. Who is Robbie referring to when he talks about 'National Treasure'? By default, you would think it speaks for itself. Being one of the UK's biggest stars, the singer could claim the title, rightfully so. But is it himself that he is referring to here?

When the song was released in 2014, we had several reasons to believe that 'National Treasure' was referring to David Bowie. First of all, Robbie seems to allude to Bowie in this ('The famous Mr. Jones'), and Bowie's real name is David Robert Jones. The lyrics read: 'He really should relax. He's due a heart attack', and we know that David Bowie had a heart attack in 2004. Another sentence, 'In a world full of weird, you're the oddest ever', appears to be a reference to Bowie's second album, *Space Oddity*. The sentence 'He can never pass as straight' would be a reference to the singer's bisexuality. The title of the song, 'National Treasure', is said to come from a 2013 interview, in which David Bowie said he was a national treasure.

However, a few days after David Bowie's death in January 2016, Robbie wanted to deny this hypothesis. On his official website, the singer said: 'I can assure you it's not David Bowie, and I can't tell you who it is, because he's someone I like, and the song isn't that flattering'. But should we believe Robbie? In the same discussion, he also indicated that he did not want to talk too much about David Bowie's death: 'Some people are angry if you do not react publicly. I find it confusing. I am not a mayor, neither a king nor a head of state.... 10 people died in Turkey yesterday. Is it more or less important than the death of David Bowie?'

It would appear that Robbie did not want to be accused of profiting over Bowie's death, and if he confessed that his song was really about Bowie, there would be a strong chance that the media would attack him for such a thing. As Robbie stated, the lyrics are not very flattering; he talks about an often-late celebrity who has reportedly suffered a heart attack in the past, who is quite strange, and who takes drugs. At a time when the world paid homage to David Bowie, Robbie does not necessarily want to let know that this title with the controversial lyrics is about the interpreter of *Blackstar*.

Musically, 'National Treasure' has it all. Helped by a strongly present piano, Robbie sings the lyrics with a retro air that is somewhat reminiscent of *Johnny English*. The song unfolds like a narrator telling a story, in a rather joyful and light atmosphere.

'Super Tony'

Writers: Robbie Williams, Kelvin Andrews Mould, Daniel Spencer Mould, Richard Scott, Scott Ralph
Duration: 3:23

The song was originally titled 'Cocaine', and Robbie released a demo of the track in 2011 as part of his *Rudebox Radio* program. Later, he decided to rename this song in 'Super Tony', and in studio version this time, on the album *Under the Radar: Volume 1* in 2014. Apart from this anecdote, the song has no other interest. Reading the lyrics, one wonders if the song was not written at the time when Robbie was precisely under the influence of drugs.

'Greenlight'

Writers: Robbie Williams, Tim Metcalfe, Flynn Francis
Duration: 3:35

'Bullet'

Writers: Robbie Williams, Tim Metcalfe, Flynn Francis
Duration: 3:49

Volume 2

'Satellites'

Writers: Robbie Williams, Stuart Price
Duration: 4:07

'9 to 5'

Writers: Dolly Parton
Duration: 3:40

'Ms Pepper'

Writers: Robbie Williams, Tim Metcalfe, Flynn Francis
Duration: 4:02

'Bambi'

Writers: Robbie Williams, Tim Metcalfe, Piers Baron
Duration: 3:21

'Eyes on the Highway'

Writers: Robbie Williams, Tim Metcalfe, Piers Baron
Duration: 4:20

'Speaking Tongues'

Writers: Robbie Williams, Johnny McDaid, Ellis Taylor
Duration: 3:37

According to the singer, the song 'Speaking Tongues' is about the time when Robbie was with Take That, in 1993 or 1994. In an interview, the singer explains that during the recording of the album *Nobody Else*, he took advantage of three days off to get to Ibiza. After a few adventures in Ibiza, Robbie flew back to Manchester, and he says that once he arrived at Gary Barlow's, he was so exhausted that he slept for two nights in a row in Gary's bed.

Robbie brings this track closer to the song 'Me and My Monkey' which also tells a story. According to the lyrics of the song, in Ibiza Robbie would have met the band Diamond Dogs: 'I met up with some boys they called themselves the diamond dogs'. However, we know that there really is a band called the Diamond Dogs—a Swedish band that was formed in the early '90s. Be careful not to confuse it with the director duo, Diamond Dogs, who produced the music video for 'You Know Me'!

Later in the song, the singer of 'Angels' is critical about the boy band's name Take That; he implies here that the name of the band is an incitement to take drugs: 'Everybody's sayin' take that, take that/And I'm about to do exactly that-ah'. The musical style of the song is very reminiscent of that of the *Rudebox* album. We come across rap, a bad boy atmosphere, and a certain lightness.

'Go Mental'

Writers: Robbie Williams, Big Narstie, Stuart Price, Felix Buxton, Atlantic Horns
Duration: 3:27

'Go Mental' is a particularly joyful song, which quickly encourages dancing. The track has never been sung live, which is a shame as it is perfectly cut for the stage. Moreover, the official clip alternates unpublished images with images of the 2017 tour.

The spirit of the song is simple: to suggest dance, celebration, and madness, thanks to dynamic music, propelled by trumpets, and accompanied by festive lyrics. We imagine very well what a live performance could give when Robbie sings these words: 'From the left to the right/To the people down below/Are you having a good time/Or do you just not know/From the front to the back/Sing along with me'.

The song is very reminiscent of another Robbie track: 'Goin' Crazy', released in 2013; the theme of madness and the presence of rap ('Goin' Crazy' featured Dizzee Rascal, while 'Go Mental' featured rapper Big Narstie). But above all, what we remember from 'Go Mental' is the controversy over its recording. Indeed, originally, Robbie wanted Shirley Bassey to feature on the song. The problem was that rapper Big Narstie bragged about it in the media, even before the recording with Shirley took place. Robbie says:

> We went into the studio together and we did a song. It was great but it didn't make the album. The song is with Basement Jaxx and I was going to get Shirley Bassey to sing on it, but then Big Narstie comes in and we have the best day. The he does an interview with *The Sun* and tells them that Shirley Bassey is on it! Then Shirley Bassey's lawyers get hold of us saying that Shirley's really upset and it has caused a problem. I'm like, 'Oh, Big Narstie, don't do that'.

In the end, 'Go Mental' is a real success: the song brings together Robbie, Big Narstie, Atlantic Horn, and Stuart Price in production.

'Run It Wild'

Writers: Robbie Williams, Tim Metcalfe, Flynn Francis, Philipp Steinke
Duration: 3:43

'Run It Wild' was recorded in 2012, during the recording sessions for the album *Take the Crown*. The track, not having been retained, was put aside to finally end up on *Volume 2* of *Under the Radar*. Also of note is that the studios of Robbie's former home in Los Angeles were named Run It Wild Studios in homage to this song. Robbie later sold this house. The interest of the song is mainly due to its music video, in which we see the singer getting a new tattoo.

'Numb'

Writers: Robbie Williams, Steve Robson, Ed Drewett
Duration: 4:02

'Andy Warhol'

Writers: Robbie Williams, Karl Brazil, Benjamin Roy Castle
Duration: 3:59

Another particularly joyful and catchy track. Growing up in the '70s and '80s, Robbie was no stranger to the cultural movements of his childhood. One of the most influential movements was pop art, a style of art for which Andy Warhol was widely known. Here is a song dedicated to him.

The lyrics of this song are particularly explicit, and they describe Warhol's universe very well. Robbie thus evokes Warhol, but also David Bowie, Tom Ford, and Studio 54, one of the high places of New York nights. To get an idea of the atmosphere of the song, it is probably enough to look at this verse: 'We're with Andy Warhol at Studio 54/That's right, ah ha, oh yeah/The boys are with the boys/ And the girls are naked on the floor/That's right, ah ha, oh yeah'.

'My Fuck You to You'

Writers: Robbie Williams, Fil Eisler
Duration: 3:42

'Weakness'

Writers: Robbie Williams, Gary Barlow
Duration: 4:15

'Booty Call'

Writers: Robbie Williams, Kelvin Andrews Mould, Daniel Spencer Mould, Scott Ralph, Richard Scott
Duration: 2:56

'On the Fence'

Writers: Robbie Williams, Kelvin Andrews Mould, Scott Ralph, Richard Scott
Duration: 3:06

'International Entertainment'

Writers: Robbie Williams, Tim Metcalfe, Piers Baron
Duration: 3:23

Volume 3

'The Impossible'

Writers: Robbie Williams, Guy Chambers
Duration: 4:34

'Gold'

Writers: Robbie Williams, Karl Brazil, Benjamin Roy Castle
Duration: 3:57

'Dirty Rotten'

Writers: Robbie Williams, Karl Brazil, Benjamin Roy Castle
Duration: 3:35

'Good People'

Writers: Robbie Williams, Stuart Price
Duration: 4:30

'Indestructible'

Writers: Robbie Williams, Guy Chambers, Crystal Waters, Neal Conway
Duration: 4:06

*'No F**ks'*

Writers: Robbie Williams, Guy Chambers
Duration: 3:34

'Underkill'

Writers: Robbie Williams, Richard Scott, Kelvin Andrews Mould, Scott Ralph
Duration: 3:35

'Bye Bye'

Writers: Robbie Williams, Karl Brazil, Benjamin Roy Castle
Duration: 3:38

'Reality Killed the Video Star'

Writers: Robbie Williams
Duration: 3:30

When in 2009, Robbie returned to the studio after a three-year absence, he recorded the album *Reality Killed the Video Star*, a title chosen as a nod to Trevor Horn's famous hit, 'Video Killed the Radio Star'.

The idea of this album title, *Reality Killed the Video Star*, is actually much older; in fact, in May 2005, Robbie had recorded a song with the same title. Although this song would give the name of the album he would release four years later, he decided not to include it. Here it is, finally, fourteen years later, in 2019, on the third volume of the *Under the Radar* series. It is one of the few songs that Robbie wrote entirely on his own, without the help of any composer.

It is interesting to note that this song definitely inspired him a lot. Indeed, in addition to the fact that he gave the name to one of his albums, Robbie also used part of the lyrics of 'Reality Killed the Video Star' to write later, in 2010, the track 'Shame' with the collaboration of Gary Barlow.

In 'Reality Killed the Video Star', we can hear these words: 'My face will be 30 foot high on the back of that bus/And on my poster they'll spray knob head at the back of Toys'R'Us'. In the song 'Shame', the idea of the poster with his effigy behind the famous toy store is mentioned again: 'Oh, and with your poster 30 foot high at the back of Toy-R-Us'. Amazing, right?

'I Just Want People to Like Me'

Writers: Robbie Williams, Tim Metcalfe, Flynn Francis
Duration: 3:14

'The National Anthem of Robbie'

Writers: Robbie Williams, Guy Chambers, Edward Elgar
Duration: 2:40

It is not really a song, and Robbie does not sing on it: this is the musical intro that played at the start of every concert on The Heavy Entertainment Show Tour in 2017. This fairly short piece (2:40) takes up the melody of the British national anthem, 'God Save the Queen', to adapt it to Robbie's persona. A choir interprets lyrics whose meaning is much more vulgar and provocative: 'He can swing like a bastard' and 'Yes he went to rehab/Drugs and drink took him low/But would still make Rudebox'. Suffice to say that the irreverent tone of this piece would shock the queen!

The presence of this track on the album *Under the Radar: Volume 3* has somewhat disturbed the fans, because it has nothing to do with the style of the album. But we can still appreciate the fact that Robbie agreed to publish the studio version of this unreleased song.

18

'Freedom' and 'United'

In a singer's discography, there are always songs that you never know where to classify, and Robbie is no exception to this rule.

Besides the many B-sides that the singer has given us over the years, some songs are neither B-sides nor taken from albums. This is the case for two songs: 'Freedom', the singer's first solo single, and 'United', released only in promo and having been used in the Pepsi advertising campaign in 2000.

'Freedom'

Writers:	George Michael
Duration:	4:20
Single release date:	29 July 1996
Charts:	No. 2 in UK

A year after leaving Take That, Robbie needed time to fully begin his solo career, so he decided to cover the famous George Michael hit 'Freedom'. This choice is undoubtedly very logical, and certainly the best possible one he could have made. Aside from the fact that 'Freedom' is a hit (not so much in terms of sales, but more in terms of image and cultural impact), it is also a track composed by Robbie's counterpart, George Michael. Like him, he comes from a boy band (Take That for Robbie and Wham! for George), and like him, he is British. Finally, it was clever for Robbie to choose a song that speaks of freedom, a year after his split from the band.

For the record, when Robbie shot the music video for the song in Miami, he did not finish recording it. For the purposes of filming, the singer used George Michael's version to be able to sing in playback on it.

If some may have been sceptical of Robbie's potential to be able to have a solo career—after all, the choice of a cover can indeed cause trouble—the ex-Take That member still managed to climb to No. 2 in the UK Singles Chart, while George only reached No. 28 in 1990. Robbie had undoubtedly been carried by those nostalgic for Take That (when the single was released, Take That had been separated for five months).

Subsequently, Robbie decided to skip performing 'Freedom' in most of his concerts. It was not until 2015 that he decided to include it again in his set lists. Even though fans do not give this song a lot of credit, since he is not the author, it still keeps the audience happy when they sing it, especially since many Robbie fans also enjoy the songs of George Michael.

'United'

Writers: Robbie Williams, Guy Chambers
Duration: 5:56

'United' is arguably an anomaly to the singer's discography. In 2000, when Robbie was about to release his third solo album, the singer signed an exclusive deal with the Pepsi brand for a massive advertising campaign. At the time, Pepsi was on the rise, and the brand continued to offer the services of the biggest stars of the day to promote their drink.

In 2000, it was Robbie's turn. In addition to finding his face on the cans and bottles of the brand, the singer offered Pepsi a new song, entitled 'United', and what a song! Although this track was never released as a single, it is as strong as some of the King of Pop's greatest nuggets.

We are dealing with a rock track whose genes are reminiscent of 'Let Me Entertain You' or those of the recent 'It's Only Us'. The track alternates calm, spoken-sung passages with much more rock passages. Beyond the quality of the song, it has also been noted that Robbie skilfully places the brand's slogan in this sentence: 'Spread some love and ask for more'.

What appeals to me the most about this song is its structure: first calm verses, then a surge; the track gains strength, before falling back. Then, after a short pause, believing the song to be over, it resumes, accompanied by sexy backing vocals and a quickening rhythm. The singer repeats over and over: 'Are we united?/Are we united?/Hey hey hey'. Finally, it ends with a conclusion orchestrated by strong percussions which accompany Robbie's voice towards its end.

Some remixes have also been released on promos. No single has been released commercially, and no music videos have been made, other than a commercial. As far as I know, Robbie only performed this song once or twice on TV during the advertising campaign, and thereafter the track was never performed on tour. It is to be regretted that such a nugget did not have a better destiny, as it would certainly have met with incredible success on tour.

19

Original Soundtracks

Like most artists of his time, Robbie was often approached to assist in the recording of film soundtracks. However, the context of these recordings often varies; in some cases, the singer only selected an already existing song from his repertoire for it to be included in the soundtrack of a film (this is the case for example of 'Beyond the Sea' and 'Summertime'), while in other cases, Robbie has recorded an unreleased track especially for the occasion ('A Man for All Seasons' and 'It's De-lovely'). Finally, in some situations, it is quite ambiguous. For example, the track 'Misunderstood' was released at the same time on his *Greatest Hits* and on the soundtrack of *Bridget Jones: The Edge of Reason*; we do not know if the singer already knew that the track would be included on the soundtrack when he recorded it.

'Not of this Earth'

Writers: Robbie Williams, Guy Chambers
Duration: 4:41

Taken from the *Bridget Jones's Diary* movie soundtrack. It was in 2001 that Robbie first participated in the release of a film soundtrack. For *Bridget Jones's Diary*—which was to be a huge success—Robbie recorded two songs: 'Have You Met Miss Jones?' (which contrary to what one might think is not an original song, but a cover) and 'Not of this Earth'. While 'Have You Met Miss Jones?' was also included on the singer's first swing album, *Swing When You're Winning*, 'Not of this Earth' is only present on this soundtrack. Also note: the soundtrack of the film had a second volume, which contains the hit 'Angels'. 'Not of this Earth' was written by Robbie and Guy Chambers. It is a swing-sounding track, just like 'Have You Met Miss Jones?'. The song sounds like a poetic and tender tribute describing the film's main character, Bridget.

'We Are the Champions'

Writers: Freddie Mercury
Duration: 3:52

Taken from *A Knight's Tale* movie soundtrack. In 2001, Robbie recorded with the band Queen a cover of the famous Freddie Mercury hit 'We Are the Champions'. It is hard to know exactly how this rather unexpected collaboration came about. What we do know, however, is that Brian May and Robbie did not just record this cover together. Indeed, Brian took the opportunity to perform a guitar solo on the track 'Eternity', recorded at the same time.

We also know that following Robbie's vocal performance on this cover, Brian May and Roger Taylor were so impressed that they proposed to the former Take That member to join the band. Rumours circulated in this direction for a while before Robbie ended up rejecting the proposal. It was finally singer Adam Lambert who accepted the deal a few years later.

We also note the participation of guitarist Billy Morrison (Camp Freddie/Billy Idol) in the recording of the song, as well as his presence in the filming of the video. In addition, Billy and Robbie were often seen together on the streets of Los Angeles at the time.

The music video, moreover, is particularly astonishing and surreal. With the story of *A Knight's Tale* set in the Middle Ages, Robbie and his accompanying musicians don period outfits. Sometimes disguised as a knight, sometimes as a king, Robbie here wears long hair, a look his audiences are not used to.

Robbie rarely sings his soundtrack songs live, but 'We Are the Champions' is an exception. As a big fan of Queen, he does not hesitate to perform it many times, just like 'We Will Rock You'. Likewise, in 2015, Robbie included 'Bohemian Rhapsody' in the set list of his concerts.

'Summertime'

Writers: Robbie Williams, Antony Genn
Duration: 4:45

Taken from the *Mike Bassett: England Manager* movie soundtrack. This is a song that lives up to its name! Indeed, the song title suggests summer, and listening to it, it is indeed a summer feeling that emerges—a strong impression of lightness and of an idyllic world.

'Summertime' first appeared on the British film soundtrack *Mike Bassett: England Manager* in 2001, but the track must have been written (and maybe even recorded) long before, as it is composed by Robbie and Antony Genn. We know that the two men mainly worked together around 1995–1996, just after Robbie left Take That and just before the singer joined Guy Chambers in 1997.

Moreover, musically, this song sounds very '90s with an electro feeling and a mid-tempo rhythm cadenced in the style of the songs of George Michael. The song is very well suited to the style of movie soundtracks. Over the minutes, the song grows in power and even contains a little rap—undoubtedly the singer's first rap verses, many years before 'Rock DJ' or 'Supreme'.

As the film *Mike Bassett: England Manager* was not exactly a must-see movie, the track went rather unnoticed in 2001. It is probably for this reason that the singer decided to re-record it in 2006 for his *Rudebox* album. For this new version, Robbie called on William Orbit for production. Incidentally, the length of the track was extended—we go from a song of 4:45 to a version of 5:42. The choice of William Orbit is no accident; on the one hand, he already produced another track from the album, 'Louise', and on the other hand, William Orbit is an electro specialist (having produced numerous Madonna songs). Suddenly, 'Summertime' having electro origins, it went without saying that this characteristic had to be retained and even amplified in 2006.

But you can tell Robbie really likes this song, as it was used again in 2012 to illustrate one of his advertising campaigns for his ready-to-wear brand, Farrell.

We notice that the singer loves to recycle some tracks; indeed, it has happened at least three times. Apart from 'Summertime' which had two versions five years apart, we also have the song 'Sexed Up', first released as a demo and B-side of the single 'No Regrets' in 1998, before becoming a separate full-length single on the *Escapology* album four years later; and the track 'Soul Transmission', first released as a B-side on the single 'Different' in 2012, before ending up on the album *The Christmas Present* in 2019. As we can see, the three songs have one thing in common: first released discreetly on a soundtrack or as B-side, they are then put forward when they end up on an album.

'A Man for All Seasons'

Writers: Robbie Williams, Hans Zimmer
Duration: 3:59

Taken from the *Johnny English* movie soundtrack. Who other than Robbie, to whom we owe the very judicious hit 'Millennium'—inspired by the James Bond movies—could better interpret a song from a movie parodying the secret agent? On the film's release, Robbie offered his talents to the very famous Hans Zimmer, to whom we owe a lot of film music.

The fruit of this collaboration: 'A Man for All Seasons', which was played during the credits of *Johnny English*. It is easy to see Hans Zimmer's talent here, with how he seamlessly adapts to the theme of a film in order to offer music that fits perfectly. It is also a song that fits perfectly with Robbie's style.

Rather cheerful, 'A Man for All Seasons' offers a dynamic melody, where words and phrases flow together with a bluffing naturalness. We also noted in the lyrics, several fairly explicit nods to Agent 007: 'When others would leak it, his service is secret' and 'His word his bond, whether brunette or blonde'.

'It's De-Lovely'

Writers: Cole Porter
Duration: 2:58

Taken from the *De-Lovely* movie soundtrack. Robbie sticks again to swing music to offer us this new track for the film: 'It's De-Lovely', for the film *De-Lovely*. But Robbie did not just perform this Cole Porter cover. Indeed, it was also the occasion for him to make his debut in the cinema; in the film, Robbie indeed makes a short appearance to play the role of a singer who sings this song during a wedding.

While the film did not stand out, Robbie still promoted the song during a performance on the American TV show *The Tonight Show with Jay Leno*.

'Collision of Worlds'

Writers: Robbie Williams, Brad Paisley
Duration: 3:49

Taken from the *Cars 2* movie soundtrack. While Robbie had participated in no less than six soundtracks in four years (between 2001 and 2004), it took seven years to see the singer return to the soundtrack of a film. It was the 3D computer-animated comedy film *Cars 2* that had this honour, with the track 'Collision of Worlds', a duet recorded with country singer Bad Paisley.

Although 'Collision of Worlds' is not really a country song, it does have some very American rock tones—no wonder for a song supposed to accompany the release of an American film produced by Disney. Not much is known about the origin of this meeting between the two artists. It is likely that their meeting and their collaboration was suggested by the producers of the film, who were looking for two sure values for this soundtrack.

'Collision of Worlds' is pretty well written. We have in front of us two singers (Robbie and Brad) who are supposed to sing about the theme of racing cars. From there emerges an obvious idea: the duet becomes a duel between the United States represented here by Brad and his country world, and the United Kingdom, represented by Robbie, and all the words of the song faithfully transmit this permanent good-child confrontation.

Indeed, the two men oppose a whole series of symbols of the two countries, as for example in this verse: 'Abbey Road, Route 66/CIA to the MI-6, right lane, left lane/Metric, imperial, pounds, dollars/Howdy, cheerio/That V-8 growl to a V-12 scream/Hail to the Chief, well, God save the Queen!' There is no need to go into more detail on this verse.

It is regrettable, however, that this song never had a performance on stage. The meeting between the two artists was limited to a recording session in the studio, images of which are available in the clip that accompanied the film's release. The nice fight between the two, reinforced by a very rock sound, could have given rise to beautiful staging in concert.

'Let's Go All the Way'

Writers: Gary "Mudbone" Cooper
Duration: 4:31

Taken from the *Iron Man 3* movie soundtrack. We will not spend too much time on this song. Originally, 'Let's Go All the Way' was a 1985 song by American band Sly Fox. In 1999, The Wondergirls decided to record a cover of the track. Among the band members is Ashley Hamilton, a friend of Robbie's. The two had already worked together on the single 'Come Undone' in 2003. At the same time, Robbie had also offered him the track 'Wimmin'' (whose demo dates from 2001). Later, Ashley was involved in writing the song 'She's Madonna', but Robbie forgot to put her name in the copyright.

Ashley did not hold a grudge, since, in 2013, they decide to re-record the song 'Let's Go All the Way' for the soundtrack of *Iron Man 3*. The track is quite noisy, and to be honest, it is very difficult to distinguish Robbie's voice on this track.

'Good Day Sunshine'

Writers: Paul McCartney, John Lennon
Duration: 1:58

Taken from the *Beat Bugs* animated children's TV series. It is not really a movie soundtrack, but a song incorporated into the *Beat Bugs* animated children's TV series released in 2016 on Netflix. Not only does Robbie provide the voice of the character 'Mr. Sun' in this cartoon, but in addition, he performs a cover of the Beatles' 'Good Day Sunshine'. Aimed at children, this song is rather cheerful and simplistic.

20

Featurings

Over the years, Robbie has shown great generosity. In addition to the fact that in the space of twenty-two years, he recorded twelve studio albums, he participated in no less than thirty-one collaborative projects, which can be grouped under the name 'featurings'. By featurings, I do not necessarily mean 'duets' but rather 'solo or duo appearance on various projects'.

'There Are Bad Times Just Around the Corner'

Writers: Noel Coward

Taken from the album *20th Century Blues*. It is arguably one of Robbie's strangest and most misunderstood songs. In 1998, he recorded a cover of 'There Are Bad Times Just Around the Corner', a track originally performed by songwriter Noel Coward. Where it is quite astonishing is that this blues-style song is readapted by Robbie in a rather electro style.

'I Started a Joke'

Writers: Bee Gees
Duration: 4:27

Taken from the album *Gotta Get a Message to You*. After the homage to Noel Coward, Robbie participated in the Bee Gees tribute album, *Gotta Get a Message to You*. He occasionally recorded a cover of the Bee Gees' 'I Started a Joke', with the English band The Orb. Here too, we are facing an electro experience, but this time accompanied by slightly reggae sounds. This version is a far cry from the original version, which was much more refined and much more classic.

'Are You Gonna Go My Way'

Writers: Lenny Kravitz, Craig Ross
Duration: 3:27

Taken from the album *Reload*. Who has not swayed their hips to Lenny Kravitz's greatest hit, 'Are You Gonna Go My Way'? When Tom Jones decided in 1999 to release his cover album, *Reload*, he called on the best artists of the day, and it was Robbie who joined him to perform the Lenny Kravitz hit as a duet. But the two men are not on their first attempt. A few months before, Robbie and Tom had already met on stage at the Brit Awards ceremony to perform together the medley known as the 'Full Monty medley'. Subsequently, they worked together again in 2012 on the track 'On My Own', the B-side of the single 'Different'.

'Loveboat/Your Disco Needs You/Kids'

Writers: Robbie Williams, Guy Chambers, Kylie Minogue

Taken from the album *Light Years*. In 2000, Kylie Minogue was about to make her comeback, and for the occasion, the Australian beauty called on Robbie and Guy Chambers to give her a helping hand. Aside from the track 'I'm So High', which does not feature Robbie but is written by Guy Chambers, three other tracks were composed by the 'Angels' singer and Guy Chambers: 'Kids', 'Loveboat', and 'Your Disco Needs You'.

'Kids', as we know, was released simultaneously on the albums of Kylie and Robbie. On the other hand, we often tend to forget the role of the singer on the album *Light Years*. While he participates only in the writing of 'Loveboat', his involvement is much more important on the gay anthem, 'Your Disco Needs You'. Robbie not only helped with the songwriting, but he is also featured on the backing vocals. Years later, he said he wanted to record his own version of 'Your Disco Needs You'. We hope this project will be successful.

'That Old Black Magic'

Writers: Johnny Mercer, Harold Arlen
Duration: 3:12

Taken from the album *The Further Adventures of Little Voice*. A year before the release of his album *Swing When You're Winning*, Robbie was already venturing into swing style when he sang Frank Sinatra's song 'That Old Black Magic'; it is on Jane Horrocks's album *The Further Adventures of Little Voice* that this duo comes to life. We have a lot of pleasure to listen to this charming light song which associates the very sexy voice of Robbie with that of Jane whose certain accents recall those of the voice of Marilyn Monroe. The two artists met again a year later on the stage of the Royal Albert Hall, where they performed the song 'Things' together.

'Sweet Gene Vincent'

Writers: Ian Dury, Chas Jankel
Duration: 4:08

Taken from the album *Brand New Boots and Panties*. We find here a new tribute: this time, Robbie honours the memory of singer Ian Dury. The song itself is another tribute to Gene Vincent (the original singer), of which Ian Dury was a fan.

For the record, Robbie and Ian met on a UNICEF trip a few months before Ian died. 'Sweet Gene Vincent' was recorded with The Blockheads, of which Ian was the frontman. Rare enough to point out: while Robbie rarely sings his featurings on stage, he nevertheless gave a live performance of this track during the musical show *Later with Jools Holland*.

'You're the Why'

Writers: Ian Dury
Duration: 4:30

Taken from the album *Ten More Turnips from the Tips*. Robbie did not settle for the track 'Sweet Gene Vincent' to pay homage to Ian Dury. He set the scene again a few months later, recording a cover of the track 'You're the Why', for the album *Ten More Turnips from the Tips*. While *Brand New Boots and Panties* was a tribute album, *Ten More Turnips from the Tips* is the last album composed by Ian Dury.

Originally, 'You're the Why' was to be sung by Ian, but he was so ill he was unable to do it. Chas Jankel had recorded a version of the track, and it was this version that was released at Ian Dury's funeral. Present at the funeral, Robbie then offered to record his own version, which can be found on the last track of the album.

'My Culture'

Writers: Robbie Williams, Duncan Philip Bridgeman, Jamie Catto, Maxi Jazz, Nigel Butler
Released as a single: 8 April 2002
Duration: 5:40
Charts: No. 9 in UK

Taken from the album *1 Giant Leap*. In 2001, two artists (Duncan Philip Bridgeman and Jamie Catto) decided to form a band by the name of 1 Giant Leap. They then recorded their first album, the eponymous *1 Giant Leap*. On this album, the two men feature many guest stars, including Michael Stipe, Dennis Hopper, Brian Eno, Neneh Cherry, and Robbie Williams. The latter records a song called 'My Culture', in duet with Maxi Jazz of the band Faithless.

'My Culture' is a song with electro sounds. The first part of the song (until 1:55) is performed by Maxi Jazz (Robbie is only present in the backing vocals). Then, Robbie becomes the main singer in the second part, and interestingly, he covers part of the poem 'Hello Sir' (available on his first solo album *Life thru a Lens*) to which he adds new verses here.

In the 'My Culture' music video, Robbie appears on the TV screen as a sixty-year-old man. This man represents his father, the one he spoke to in 'Hello Sir'. After a few seconds, his father realises that it is his son he is seeing on TV. Robbie, in a modest grey striped sweater, appears to be in a suburban neighbourhood. He raps in front of buildings that eventually take off and reach space.

'My Culture' met with some success, as without any real promotion, the single still ranked No. 9 on the UK Singles Chart.

'Wimmin"

Writers: Robbie Williams, Ashley Hamilton
Released as a single: 2 June 2003
Duration: 3:10
Charts: No. 27 in UK

During the 2001 winter tour, Robbie fans discovered an unreleased track: 'Women'. While fans were hoping for a studio version of this new release soon, Robbie finally decided to gift the song to Ashley Hamilton, who had been involved in writing it anyway. The track became 'Wimmin", and Ashley ended up releasing it as a single in June 2003. On the version sung by Ashley, Robbie is featured in the backing vocals, including the song's various 'Wow'.

'Do They Know It's Christmas'

Writers: Bob Geldof, Midge Ure
Released as a single: 29 November 2004
Duration: 5:07
Charts: No. 1 in UK

The UK is a big fan of charity events, and the music world is no different. As one of the main representatives of Britpop, Robbie is therefore regularly contacted to participate in the recording of charity singles. This is the case here, with a new version of the song 'Do They Know It's Christmas', written by Bob Geldof and Midge Ure.

The first version was recorded in 1984, during the famine crisis that rocked Ethiopia between 1983 and 1985. Bob Geldof therefore took the initiative, twenty years later, to re-record the song with a new series of artists, of which Robbie was one. A music video, showing the different singers in the studio, is also produced. As in 1984, the single again ranked No. 1 in the UK Singles Chart.

'Jealousy'

Writers: Chris Lowe, Neil Tennant
Duration: 5:57

Taken from the album *Concrete*. The friendship between the Pet Shop Boys and Robbie is well established. Their first collaboration took place during the recording of the single 'No Regrets' in 1998. We also know of their collaboration on the single 'She's Madonna' in 2006. At the same time, the Pet Shop Boys invited Robbie to join them on stage during a unique concert given on 8 May 2006 at the Mermaid Theater in London in front of 600 fans. On this occasion, Robbie sang one of the hits of the English duo: 'Jealousy'. A few months later, the Pet Shop Boys released the double live album, *Concrete*, on which we find the live performance of 'Jealousy', sung by Robbie.

'The Only One I Know'

Writers: Martin Blunt, Tim Burgees, Jon Brookes, Rob Collins, Jonathan Baker
Duration: 4:00

Taken from the album *Version*. The encounter between Robbie and Mark Ronson is arguably one of the best of his career. The two men got to know each other around 2006, when Robbie recorded his album *Rudebox*. At the time, Mark Ronson was one of the most famous producers of the day, and all the biggest artists were snapping up, starting with Amy Winehouse.

Several months after the release of *Rudebox*, Robbie worked again with Mark, recording the cover album *Version*, which also featured Lily Allen and Amy Winehouse. Together, Robbie and Mark recorded the cover of 'The Only One I Know', a song by The Charlatans. The track is not released as a single, but the album has been ranked No. 2 on the Top Albums Chart.

'Please Don't Talk About Me When I'm Gone'

Writers: Sam H. Stept, Sidney Clare
Duration: 4:00

Taken from the album *Forever Cool*. Twelve years after Dean Martin's death, Capitol Records released an album of posthumous duets, titled *Forever Cool*. For the production of this posthumous album, Dean Martin's real voice is used for the recording of unreleased duets between him and contemporary artists, such as Kevin Spacey, Joss Stone, Charles Aznavour, and Robbie.

Once again, Robbie therefore highlights his talents as a swing singer on the track 'Don't Talk About Me When I'm Gone', which he sings in duet with Dean Martin. It is impressive how easily Robbie used his crooning skills. Robbie is not his first attempt in terms of a fictional duo, since he had already tried the experience on the track 'It was a Very Good Year', in the company of Frank Sinatra, virtually present on the stage of the Royal Albert Hall in 2001.

'Lola'

Writers: Ray Davies
Duration: 4:11

Taken from the album *Radio 1: Established 1967*. For the fortieth anniversary of BBC Radio, the famous radio station offered a compilation of covers, performed by the best artists of the moment, to retrace the four decades of its history. This compilation, in the form of a double album, is titled *Radio 1: Established 1967* and was released in shops on 1 October 2007. The concept is very simple: the album, made up of forty songs classified in chronological order, traces the history of British music between 1967 and 2007.

For the year 1970, it is Robbie who sticks to it: the singer offers to the BBC his version of the track 'Lola', a song by the band The Kinks. The song is produced by Guy Chambers. Sorry? But we thought the two men were no longer talking to each other? Unless the track has been recorded several years before, 'Lola' is the first collaboration between Guy and Robbie since 2002. We saw later that their reunion took place mainly from 2012, during concerts at the O2 in London.

Subsequently, 'Lola' can be found on CD 3 of the compilation *In and Out of Consciousness*. This CD brings together several B-sides recorded in the past.

'Everybody Hurts'

Writers: Bill Berry, Peter Buck, Mick Mills, Michael Stipe
Duration: 5:26
Released as a single: 7 February 2010
Charts: No. 1 in UK

Following the earthquake that rocked Haiti on 12 January 2010, British Prime Minister Gordon Brown asked Simon Cowell to set up the recording of a charity single. He then chose R.E.M.'s famous hit, 'Everybody Hurts'. The song was recorded in the days that followed, and the single was released on 7 February 2010. Robbie is therefore one of the artists participating in the project, alongside Rod Stewart, Mariah Carey, Mika, Kylie Minogue, and Gary Barlow, to name a few. A stunning black and white music video was shot.

The singer's commitment to Haiti does not end there. He travelled to Haiti a little later, as part of a charity trip organised by UNICEF. A report was produced and broadcast during the Soccer Aid football match in June of the same year.

'Carry On'

Writers: Kai Elle, Mark Hayes, James McLaughlin
Duration: 3:47

'Carry On' is a song performed by Kai Elle, with backing vocals provided by Robbie. The lyrics were written in part by Mark Hayes, one of the singer's friends. Fun fact: Robbie recorded his game on 1 January 2012.

'ILMP (I Love My Penis)/Charity Song'

Writers: Chris Moyles, Sandy Beech, Dave Bethell
Duration: 3:51/4:36

Taken from the album *The Difficult Second Album*. You cannot count the number of times Robbie has had to go to radio station premises to promote a single or an album, and among the radio presenters he has met several times is the famous presenter Chris Moyles, who has been on numerous stations, such as BBC Radio 1 and Capital FM. Chris has one thing in common with Robbie: they were both born in February 1974 (Chris was born nine days after Robbie).

Besides his radio and TV shows, Chris has also recorded two parody albums: *The Parody Album* in 2009 and *The Difficult Second Album* in 2012. On the latter, he calls on Robbie twice: 'ILMP (I Love My Penis)' (the title says it all) and 'Charity Song'. On the latter, we also find others close to Robbie, namely Olly Murs, Gary

Barlow, and Ed Sheeran. Musically, the songs are not unpleasant to listen to, their interest lies above all in the lyrics which are only intended to make us smile.

'Muñequita Linda'

Writers: Maria Grever
Duration: 3:34

Taken from the album *Habítame Siempre*. Although Robbie is English, he never refused to try other languages when performing songs. You must admit that, most of the time, when Robbie sings in French or Spanish, it is mostly for business reasons. Thus, the Spanish version of 'Angels' and the French version of 'Supreme' were mainly recorded to reach the Hispanic and French market.

However, this is not always the case. Here, the singer has once again agreed to play the foreign language game, with the track 'Muñequita Linda', which he sings in Spanish, alongside Mexican singer Thalia. Their meeting had already taken place a few years ago, through EMI Music. In 2012, their collaboration was finally born, with 'Muñequita Linda', a pretty Spanish serenade which makes us say that Robbie has more than one string to his bow.

Of the song, Thalia said:

> With Robbie Williams it was a dream because I admire his work. I took the risk of inviting him for this song, which is a mambo made famous by Nat King Cole, 'Muñequita Linda'. I knew that the only one who could understand the irony of rescuing that He was the mambo. I sent it to him and he loved the idea and he sang in Spanish. It was spectacular.

According to a Spanish website: 'In fact, its author, the Mexican composer María Grever, dedicated this song to her daughter, who unfortunately lost when she was only a few months old'. Finally, according to another source: 'María Grever had two daughters and a son, the youngest died when she was barely six months old, that tragedy forever marked the life of María Grever and in memory of her little daughter, she wrote the song "Muñequita Linda"'.

'He Ain't Heavy, He's My Brother'

Writers: Bobby Scott, Bob Russell
Duration: 4:35
Released as a single: 17 December 2012
Charts: No. 1 in UK

Here is another charity project that Robbie was involved in. Its context is quite particular. In 1989, a mob movement at a soccer match in Sheffield resulted in the deaths of ninety-six people. Responsibility for this tragedy was first attributed to the supporters of the soccer team. But after a very long investigation which ended in 2012, it was established that the responsibility for the disaster lay with the South Yorkshire

Police (SYP). Immediately after the investigation was concluded, a charity single was commissioned, and it was this song, 'He Ain't Heavy, He's My Brother', that was chosen to raise funds for the bereaved families. A large number of musicians and artists, united under the name The Justice Collective, recorded this cover. In addition to Robbie, we find among others, Mel C of the Spice Girls and Paul McCartney. Guy Chambers is producing, while former Robbie percussionist Chris Sharrock is also in attendance. As is often the case in the UK, this new charity single immediately ranked No. 1 in sales.

'Goin' Crazy'

Writers: Dylan Mills, Robbie Williams, Tim Anderson, Jamin Wilcox
Duration: 3:24
Released as a single: 16 June 2013
Charts: No. 5 in UK

Pop, rock, swing, rap, electro—nothing stops him! Here, Robbie gets back to rap. The origin of this collaboration would be quite simple: rapper Dizzee Rascal, in the middle of recording his album *The Fifth*, must finalise the production of a song called 'Goin 'Crazy'. He first called on rapper Example to perform the chorus. But not being convinced by Example's performance, Dizzee decides to call on Robbie to replace him.

The 'Supreme' singer agreed, and when you see the music video for the song, you almost think it is a Robbie song, since he is the one opening the video. While Dizzee Rascal provides the rap part of the track, Robbie provides the rock side of the song. Filmed in the streets of London, the two artists travel a street behind the wheel of exuberant customised vehicles. Robbie is particularly noted for his jacket, the back of which features the provocative 'Megaupload' label in large print. Their collaboration was not limited to that, as Dizzee also offered to join Robbie on stage in concert, a few weeks before the single's release.

'The Days'

Writers: Tim Bergling, Al Fakir, Brandon Flowers, Vincent Pontare, Robbie Williams
Duration: 4:38
Released as a single: 3 October 2014

Taken from the album *Stories*. Originally, 'The Days' was meant to be a collaboration between Brandon Flowers (The Killers) and Avicii. But Brandon was unhappy with his work on the song, so Avicii decided to call on Robbie to provide the vocals. 'The Days' is not the only song Brandon Flowers gave to Robbie. Two years later, he also gave him 'Mixed Signals', which would become one of the singles from the album *The Heavy Entertainment Show*.

The song first appeared as the soundtrack of an advertising campaign for clothing brand Ralph Lauren in early September 2014. The song was subsequently revealed in its entirety. A lyric video was produced, as well as an official music video.

This song shines with its lightness, dynamism, melody, and freshness. It is incredibly efficient, and one can only regret its lack of use. Indeed, while the track enjoyed an EP release, its UK release as a single was cancelled. As for Robbie, who is, however, the singer on this title, he has never performed it, neither on TV set nor in concert. This situation is even more incomprehensible when you consider that, at the time, Avicii enjoyed immense popularity with young people.

However, we highlighted the extraordinary performance of its lyric video, which in 2021 reached 200 million views on YouTube. It must be said that it is rather brilliant: an artist paints the portrait of Avicii, using spray paint—what a creative visual. But again, Robbie's absence from the music video (both the lyric video and the official video) is regrettable. By the way, Robbie's name does not even appear on the EP cover.

'Bridge Over Troubled Water'

Writers: Paul Simon
Duration: 3:53
Released as a single: 21 June 2017

With each new drama, a new charity single. Following the terrible fire that ravaged the Grenfell Tower in London and claimed the lives of seventy-nine people, the decision was made to immediately record a new charity single. English producer Simon Cowell became the conductor of this operation. The result: a single recorded in record time. 'Bridge Over Troubled Water' was released on 21 June 2017, just one week after the fire!

Among the artists bringing their musical contribution, we have James Blunt, Craig David, Leona Lewis, Emeli Sandé, Dua Lipa, and, of course, Robbie Williams. A music video alternating colour images, linked to the drama and images in the studio, filmed in black and white, was also produced. Obviously, like any good self-respecting charity single, the single ranked No. 1 in the UK Singles Chart when it was released.

'Everybody Wants to Rule the World'

Writers: Roland Orzabal, Ian Stanley, Chris Hugues
Duration: 3:26

Taken from the album *Trevor Horn Reimagines the Eighties*. The best Robbie fans know that Trevor Horn is the producer of *Reality Killed the Video Star*, which marked the singer's return after three years of absence. Ten years later, in 2019, it was therefore only natural that Trevor Horn would think of Robbie again for his new album (Trevor's this time). For his album *Trevor Horn Reimagines the Eighties*, the producer summons a series of artists he appreciates to ask them to perform covers of songs from the '80s. He therefore calls on Robbie to cover the song 'Everybody Wants to Rule the World' by Tears for Fears, one of the bands Robbie grew up with.

Recorded with the 'Sarm Orchestra', the song is revealed in a new light, much to the delight of fans of Tears for Fears and Robbie. Trevor Horn was not spared by critics for this album, however, and the 'Angels' frontman is no exception. In particular, Trevor was criticised that the version, re-orchestrated in his own way, completely distorted the original. Some critics have likened the covers on the album to funeral songs. As for the performance signed by Robbie, it has been judged as too flat and disinterested.

'Electrico Romantico'

Writers: Bob Sinclar
Duration: 2:45
Released as a single: 18 January 2019

Five years after the single 'The Days' produced by the Avicii, Robbie renewed the experience, with the track 'Electrico Romantico', produced by Frenchman Bob Sinclar. It was the latter who first revealed the existence of this single, a few weeks before its official release in January 2019.

Like 'The Days', 'Electrico Romantico' enjoys incredible freshness and lightness, two qualities that come up often in dance tracks. The best producers such as David Guetta or Bob Sinclar have something to do with perfectly calibrating their creations and thus arouse intense dynamism and joie de vivre. Bob Sinclar did not hesitate to make the most of this featuring. With video teasers, remixes, marketing videos posted on social networks, and interviews, the hype was up to the quality of this song.

Once again, we can only regret the total absence of Robbie for the promotion of this track. The singer missed a golden opportunity: to reach both French audiences and young audiences, thanks to 'Electrico Romantico'. While Robbie's name does appear on the cover (unlike 'The Days'), no music video with the singer was shot.

Fortunately, we can only congratulate Bob Sinclar, who never got discouraged: nine months after the single was released, the DJ reused Robbie's voice to transform the track 'Electrico Romantico' into a new remix, this time titled 'Romantico Starlight', with the help of the Supermen Lovers. The song becomes a mashup of the songs 'Electrico Romantico' and 'Starlight' by the Supermen Lovers. A Maxi 45 RPM vinyl was produced.

'2 Become 1'

Writers: Spice Girls, Matt Rowe, Richard Stannard
Duration: 3:42

Taken from the album *My Happy Place*. Everyone remembers the Spice Girls frenzy in 1994, when their male counterparts, Take That, were also booming in the UK. Good times.

The fate of the two bands was quite similar, since in both cases, the bands dissolved before returning a few years later. Another common point: many members of the two bands ended up embarking on a solo career. Among the boys, it was mainly Robbie, Gary Barlow, and Mark Owen who embarked on the solo adventure. As for the girls, we especially remember the solo adventure of Geri Halliwell.

While Robbie is arguably the one whose solo career has been the most important, Emma Bunton does not have to be ashamed of her career. Emma, nicknamed 'Baby Spice', was not just a singer for the Spice Girls. Besides solo albums, the young woman has also ventured into television, film, and radio.

Robbie is regularly in radio studios to promote his albums, it is only natural that he found himself in the premises of Heart Radio on several occasions, in particular on the program *Heart Breakfast*, where Emma is a host. From there to the two artists working together, it was only one step away. However, their paths first crossed in 2013: then in full promotion of his album *Swings Both Ways*, Robbie invited Emma Bunton to join him on stage to sing together the song 'Dream a Little Dream of Me'. Fans loved it.

Robbie and Emma then tried it again three years later; at the end of 2016, the singer of 'Angels' invited Baby Spice to sing this time one of the greatest hits of Spice Girls: '2 Become 1'. The performance was particularly successful, and the fans exulted—all asked for a studio version of this cover.

Emma Bunton heard the voice of the fans, and again three years later, in April 2019, the young woman made their dream come true. For her album *My Happy Place*, she recorded with Robbie the studio version of '2 Become 1'. This magnificent ride is perfect for melting the hearts of Robbie and Emma fans.

'The Big Goodbye'

Writers: Robbie Williams, Martin Page
Duration: 4:32

Taken from the album *Twenty Twenty*. Besides Emma Bunton, Robbie also worked with another sidekick from the '90s: Ronan Keating of Boyzone, and like Emma, Ronan Keating became a radio host for a breakfast show. While Emma worked on Heart Radio, Ronan hosted Magic Radio at the same time. One difference, however, was that Emma and Robbie sang twice on stage before then going to the studio, whereas Ronan and Robbie were satisfied with just the studio. The two men recorded together the track 'The Big Goodbye', a song that found its way back into the studio on Ronan's album *Twenty Twenty*.

'The Big Goodbye' pays homage to Stephen Gately, the other singer of Boyzone, who died in 2009 of a pulmonary edema. The origins of this song are quite obscure. Originally, Ronan indicated that Robbie was the sole author:

> It was last year, on the 10th anniversary of Stephen's death. The guys and I were doing a TV show in London. Robbie saw the show, and he emailed me that night. He told me:
>
> 'Hey, Ro, I have this song that I wrote, and I wrote it the week Stephen died. And I'm standing in my kitchen, and I'm in tears … let's do something together, and it will be lovely.'
>
> And we worked on this record, and it's a very special song.

However, the reality is not as magical as it seems. A few months after the song's release, composer Martin Page reveals that he co-wrote the track with Robbie, and most importantly, he explains the context of his writing. Martin thus reveals that his writing was much more complex and much less spontaneous:

> I remember taking a rough home demo track up to Robbie Williams' house in Los Angeles. We'd become friends playing football at his home playing field, and kicking a ball around in the San Fernando Valley. Playing soccer together was our acquaintance.
>
> Robbie had found out about my songwriting history and by hook or crook we'd become close. This track that I took up to him had balls—fire—but also emotion. When Robbie asked me to write with him, I prepared a lot of ideas, as was my way. This concept seemed the strongest, so I shopped this vibe to Robbie with vigor. We'd been writing together for a while, jamming, checking each other out, and this rough demo of mine triggered enthusiasm in Robbie—he jumped on to writing the lyrics to my music and melodies.
>
> What was fantastic about Robbie was how he studied the phonetic vocals I sang on my demo, how he emulated my guide demo vocal. He was a master at catching the nuances. Even though I scatted and sang free-form a great deal, he wanted to totally capture the essence of my lead vocal. He was determined to get 'my' spirit of the song.
>
> I've always believed Rob to be an excellent lyricist … I told him so on many occasions—to trust his instinct. He is the king of slight of hand, of cheeky sophistication, of irony. So that was our job: ME music, ROB lyrics concept—beautiful.
>
> Luckily my very talented mate, Bobby Summerfield (who I also kicked a ball around with), agreed to produce the finished song with me at his top-of-the-line pro home studio in Sherman Oaks. We transferred my home demo to Bobby's studio, and Robbie came over to Bobby's to sing the finished item. Now —- Bobby is top notch in every way—the toppermost best … and together, he and I produced this demo.
>
> Robbie had written some sublime personal lyrics … sometimes texting them to me as he wrote them. When he sang them at Bobby's … I knew something special was going on.
>
> A few years on … Ronan Keating discovers the song via Robbie. Robbie's lyrics had come home … and Ronan records the song as a duet with Robbie on his *Twenty/Twenty*—2020 solo album. Rob's words for the late Boyzone member, Stephen Gately, are finally allowed to breathe.…
>
> Here then is the demo that I recorded with Robbie Williams. The original demo—[the music] was initially started at my home studio. I played and programmed all of the instruments, and sang guide vocal melodies and background vocals. Then I transferred my demo to Bobby Summerfield's studio so we could record Robbie's

> lead and backing vocals there. Then those tracks were sent back to my home studio—where (after adding my electric guitar solo lines) I finally mixed the finished demo you now hear. The demo is produced by myself and Bobby Summerfield.

If the words of Martin Page confirm that the song was well written many years before, and that Robbie did participate in the writing of it, it is, however, not obvious that this one was dedicated from the beginning to Stephen Gately.

Strange Days

Writers:	Luke Spiller, Jon Levine, Jed Elliot, Gethin Davies, Adam Slack
Duration:	4:53
Released as a single:	16 October 2020

Taken from the album *Strange Days*. 'Strange Days' was certainly the biggest surprise given to Robbie fans in 2020. As the world barely recovered from the first wave of COVID-19, the band The Struts decided to release a brand new track as a single—'Strange Days', featuring Robbie, recorded during the first lockdown.

This collaboration was born when The Struts launched their Radio Quarantine on Instagram Live. Robbie spontaneously showed up at one of their Instagram sessions and asked to speak one-on-one with Luke Spiller, frontman of The Struts. The two men ended up talking to each other on Facetime, bringing up many topics, such as life, music, and UFOs. Luke then offered to work with Robbie on a song, and he agreed. This is how the track 'Strange Days' was born, the lyrics inevitably reminiscent of the pandemic and the lockdown.

Sometime later, Robbie offered to come and shoot the video for the song in front of his house in Los Angeles. The result is a stunning black-and-white clip, outside the walls of the performer's house.

The song became the lead single from the album of the same name. The promotion of the single was limited to a single performance, given during the half-time of the Soccer Aid match on 6 September 2020. While the band performed it from the stadium in Manchester, Robbie appeared via hologram as he was in Switzerland.

'Stop Crying Your Heart Out'

Writers:	Noel Gallagher
Duration:	3:43
Released as a single:	13 November 2020

Robbie's interest in charity singles is well established. He is one of the artists most involved in charitable projects, whether near or far—sometimes directly involved (as is the case for example with Soccer Aid, of which he is the creator) and sometimes only a simple stakeholder.

Among all the projects in which he has worked, he has participated most with Children in Need. This time, the singer collaborated on the recording of this new charity single, 'Stop Crying Your Heart Out', a cover of a song from the band Oasis. The list of singers on this single is particularly impressive. Besides Robbie, we also find Bryan Adams, Cher, Mel C, Jamie Cullum, Lenny Kravitz, Kylie Minogue, and Nile Rodgers, to name a few.

A music video, bringing together all the stars of this song, was also produced. Due to COVID restrictions, each artist was filmed in a different location, most outdoors.

The single ranked No. 7 in the UK Singles Chart.

'If I Don't Cry (Demo)/A House Without a Mum (Demo)'

Writers: Robbie Williams, Guy Chambers, Chris Heath
Durations: 3:22/4:36

On 6 November 2017, Guy Chambers, Robbie, and Chris Heath began writing previously unreleased songs for the musical adaptation of the children's book *The Boy in the Dress*. This novel was written in 2008 by David Walliams, one of the singer's close friends. The book tells the story of a twelve-year-old boy who loves to wear dresses.

The musical was born two years later, in November 2019, in Stratford, England. A year later, in December 2020, the production decided to release a studio album containing all the songs from the show, performed by the actors. The album contains twenty-one tracks, including two sung by Robbie: 'If I Don't Cry (Demo)' and 'A House Without a Mum (Demo)'.

In fact, it is quite possible that Robbie recorded demos for each of the musical's tracks. This practice is common: when a singer writes songs to be performed by another singer or band, it is not uncommon for the singer to record a demo, in order to guide the one who will then record his own version. This is why the two songs offered here, 'If I Don't Cry' and 'A House Without a Mum', bear the indication 'demo'.

The result is extraordinary. 'If I Don't Cry' is without doubt one of the most beautiful songs written by Robbie. Accompanied only by piano, Robbie lays his voice over strong, simple, and incredibly moving lyrics. In this song, Robbie evokes the worries and fears of a twelve-year-old child faced with the departure of his mother, leaving the family home.

The second track sung by Robbie on this musical is called 'A House Without a Mum'. While the theme is the same, the loneliness of little Dennis (the main character) is approached from a different angle. If the rhythm here is much faster and inviting to dance, the lyrics are just as sad, and in the style of musicals, the song alternates falsely festive moments with sad verses. Another great track to listen to!

Epilogue

What a universe! What an impressive catalogue! Writing this book allowed me to rediscover Robbie's songs. Once again, with more than 300 original tracks and more than eighty covers, Robbie has an incredible and dense catalogue.

Robbie's solo career began over twenty-five years ago, and over the years, he has worked with most major musical genres: pop rock, electro, rock, rap, dance, and swing. He is a music lover, and as Guy Chambers says, he is obsessed with words and with writing. His writing skills and his chameleonic talents to marry the most varied musical styles are the least known of his personality, and I hope I have helped raise awareness of this aspect of his career.

I took great pleasure in re-listening to his songs, sometimes turning up the sound to better appreciate them and thus better describe them. Sometimes I rediscovered the emotions that they had already given me in the past, or even discovered new emotions. Listening, for example, to the song 'No Regrets' with the volume cranked up allowed me to appreciate all its grandeur and richness.

For a long time, I often considered that most of Robbie's B-sides deserved to be on one of his albums, I thought they were so successful. But listening to all of his songs again made me change my mind. Indeed, when we take the time to integrate the song as a whole—its lyrics, its melody, its style, its power, its structure, and its rhythm—we understand better why some tracks deserve to be released as a single, while others are destined to stay quietly on the album or end up as a B-side.

However, some choices of singles or B-sides are more than questionable. Songs that we would never have imagined as singles end up being commercially released, while some, released as B-sides, would surely have deserved a better fate.

The number of people with whom Robbie has collaborated since 1995 (we can indeed consider that his solo career began in 1995 when he frequented the band Oasis in studio) is also particularly impressive. Not only has he worked with many composers, but in addition, the singer has multiplied duets and featurings over the years with great ease. Sometimes, a simple meeting with a singer living in his neighbourhood, or in the detours of a TV studio, or an online chat leads to a new song or a new recording. This is one of the greatest paradoxes: if the public risks retaining only a handful of hits, its musical catalogue bears witness to unlimited creativity.

I hope I have made you want to immerse yourself in his songs again, to explore the lyrics more, to identify the implicit or hidden messages, and to recognise the recurring themes, but also, to have expanded your universe. Listening to Robbie's songs also means getting to know the artists with whom he has worked, such as the Pet Shop Boys, Tom Jones, Kylie Minogue, Stephen Duffy, or Trevor Horn. It is also a way to get away from clichés: yes, a pop rock singer can rap or play the crooners on swing tracks or even have fun on electro or country. Listening to songs, listening to lyrics, is to let your emotions speak, tickle the imagination, and learn to know yourself!